Queer Transgressions in Twentieth-Century Polish Fiction

Queer Transgressions in Twentieth-Century Polish Fiction

Gender, Nation, Politics

Jack J. B. Hutchens

LEXINGTON BOOKS
Lanham • Boulder • New York • London

Published by Lexington Books
An imprint of The Rowman & Littlefield Publishing Group, Inc.
4501 Forbes Boulevard, Suite 200, Lanham, Maryland 20706
www.rowman.com

6 Tinworth Street, London SE11 5AL, United Kingdom

Copyright © 2020 by The Rowman & Littlefield Publishing Group, Inc.

All rights reserved. No part of this book may be reproduced in any form or by any electronic or mechanical means, including information storage and retrieval systems, without written permission from the publisher, except by a reviewer who may quote passages in a review.

British Library Cataloguing in Publication Information Available

Library of Congress Cataloging-in-Publication Data

Names: Hutchens, Jack J. B., 1974- author.
Title: Queer transgressions in twentieth-century Polish fiction : gender, nation, politics / Jack J. B. Hutchens.
Description: Lanham : Lexington Books, 2020. | Includes bibliographical references and index.
Identifiers: LCCN 2020009428 (print) | LCCN 2020009429 (ebook) | ISBN 9781793605030 (cloth) | ISBN 9781793605054 (pbk) | ISBN 9781793605047 (epub)
Subjects: LCSH: Polish fiction--20th century--History and criticism. | Literature and society--Poland--History--20th century. | Queer theory.
Classification: LCC PG7099.3 H88 2020 (print) | LCC PG7099.3 (ebook) | DDC 891.8/5380935266--dc23
LC record available at https://lccn.loc.gov/2020009428
LC ebook record available at https://lccn.loc.gov/2020009429

Contents

Acknowledgments vii
Introduction 1

1 Iwaszkiewicz and Gombrowicz: Sex, Death, and Panic 23
2 Julian Stryjkowski: The Pole, the Jew, the Queer 51
3 Marian Pankowski: The Anti-Martyr 75
4 Olga Tokarczuk: Transgressive Bodies, Transgressing Borders 95

Conclusion 121
Epilogue: Queer Liberation in the Twenty-First Century, and Jerzy Nasierowski 125
Bibliography 131
Index 139
About the Author 143

Acknowledgments

So many people were involved in assisting me to write this book that I hesitate to call it my own. Without their gracious, untiring support it would have been nearly impossible to complete. I would like to start by thanking the American Council for Learned Societies (ACLS) for their generous research fellowship, which allowed me to travel to Poland to begin the work on this project. Through it I had access to files and texts I would not otherwise have had. It also provided me several months free from teaching, during which time I was able to make a significant start on my writing.

I would also like to thank my past colleagues in the Center for European Studies at the University of Florida. Their kindness and comradery provided me a smooth start to my professional career. Thank you as well to my students from my Queer Nations course which I taught for the first time at Florida. Their insightful discussions and comments on the texts we read led to some revisions in two of my chapters that most definitely improved my analyses. Thank you as well to my current colleagues in the Polish Studies Program at Loyola University Chicago, where I have been teaching for the past three years. They have been an endless source of support and inspiration for me since my first day there.

I was also fortunate in having the opportunity to work with some of the most supportive professors in academia during my graduate career at the University of Illinois. I would like to thank the following who kindly agreed to act as members of my dissertation committee. Professor Lilya Kaganovsky provided unendingly patient advice as well as repeated explanations of Freud over the years, for which I will always be grateful. Professor Harriet Murav allowed me to enter the Slavic Languages and Literatures program at Illinois and worked tirelessly to accommodate me in my study of Polish literature. Professor David Cooper was an unfaltering supporter of mine from the moment I started my doctoral studies, more than once agreeing to teach me through independent studies when his time was already stretched thin. He has also been an amazing editor of my work, continuously revealing the weaknesses of my less than perfect arguments, and praising the strengths in my more successful ones. Finally, I must thank Professor George Gasyna who immediately became my mentor in Polish literature when we met in 2005. Without his guidance, advice, and unwavering support my study of Polish would have ended before it even began. I cannot thank him enough for his tireless efforts on my behalf, his patient reading and re-reading of my work, and his incisive notes that made this project much more successful than it would have been without him. Thank you all so much.

None of the following work would have been possible without the love and support of my family. I must thank my parents, Jackie and Hal Hutchens for all they have done for me over the years. I would also like to thank my brothers, Hal and John Hutchens for all their love and kindness through the years.

Finally, I would like to dedicate this work to my amazing wife and best friend, Amanda Klousnitzer-Hutchens, and my beautiful daughter, Harriet. Their love and patience helped me overcome multiple creative roadblocks over the course of writing this book. I cannot imagine that I would be where I am today if not for them. Kocham was mucho!

Introduction

In 1992, a small collection entitled *Dyskretne namiętności* (Discrete Passions) was published in Poland. It was a compilation of short stories and pieces of longer works of homoerotic Polish fiction. The introduction begins with the following judgment of the presence of non-normative sexualities in Polish literature:

> Homoeroticism in Polish prose? In our society this topic belongs to the realm of the taboo, it constitutes a medium for infantile jokes, and for many, it probably smells of "pornography" or even "vulgarity." This most probably occurred due to the influence of several centuries of pressure from the moral education of the Catholic Church, and yielding to "this kind of proclivity" has been rather unbecoming in the social opinion of the Polish ethos. (Jöhling 1992, 5) [1]

A glance over the contents of this slim volume reveals an interesting truth: despite the pressures of various ideologies throughout the twentieth century to keep non-normative voices silent—whether those ideologies were fascist, communist, Catholic, or neo-liberal—there existed a vibrant, transgressive trend within Polish literature that subverted such silencing. In the work that follows, I hope to contribute to the movement of bringing discussions of non-normative identities in Poland out of the "realm of the taboo." Though this is a scholarly work, my purpose, as idealistic as it may sound, is to make an intervention into both Polish culture and politics. I wish to challenge the proliferation of nationalism and homophobia in Poland.

This study is neither one of political science, nor sociology, nor history. Its subject is literature, and while political, sociological, and historical contexts can lend insights into an analysis of literature, my chief methodology is the close reading and explication of various works of twentieth-century

Polish fiction. These analyses reveal the subversive power each work demonstrates in their transgressions of nationalist and homophobic ideologies. As my analysis is heavily influenced by Queer theory, I take for granted the fact that identities are constructed, which is nearly axiomatic in contemporary scholarship. However, rather than simply adding to the body of work on that "constructedness" of identities, whether gender or national, I investigate what results when their limits are transgressed.

In his essay "A Preface to Transgression," (1977) Michel Foucault puts forward the following definition of transgression:

> Transgression does not seek to oppose one thing to another, nor does it achieve its purpose through mockery or by upsetting the solidity of foundations; it does not transform the other side of the mirror [. . .]. Transgression is neither violence in a divided world (in an ethical world); nor victory over limits (in a dialectical or revolutionary world); and for this reason its role is to measure the excessive distance that it opens at the heart of the limit and to trace the flashing line that causes the limit to arise. Transgression contains nothing negative, but affirms limited being—affirms the limitlessness into which it leaps as it opens this zone to existence for the first time. But correspondingly, this affirmation contains nothing positive: no content can bind it, since by definition, no limit can possibly restrict it. (1977, 35–36)

Foucault sees the transgressive moment as almost accidental, as something that cannot be recognized until well past the limit, looking back. For him transgression is neither productive nor destructive; it is neither affirmation nor negation. This refusal to admit a larger degree of power to the transgressive act makes much of Foucault's assessment of transgression less useful to my project. In the works I analyze, transgression takes on a quite deliberate, politically charged character. The limit is clear, and entirely unambiguous. The act of crossing that limit is purposeful, the goal being to subvert hegemonic institutions such as, in the works I read, nationalism and heteronormativity. As Peter Stallybrass and Allon White note in *The Politics and Poetics of Transgression*, transgression acts as a "kind of reverse or counter-sublimation, undoing the discursive hierarchies and stratifications of bodies and cultures which bourgeois society has produced as the mechanism of its symbolic dominance" (1986, 201). Unlike Foucault then, Stallybrass and White see the power transgressive acts exhibit in subverting cultural norms.

Two examples of transgression being deployed as a consciously political tool are the Queer Nation movement, specifically their activities in the mid-1990s, and gay pride parades, particularly those that have taken place in Poland. In their essay "Queer Nationality," from the collection *Fear of a Queer Planet*, Lauren Berlant and Elizabeth Freeman discuss the impact the activities of the Queer Nation group have had on the politics of gay and lesbian liberation in the United States. What is especially effective in the group's program, and what has special bearing on my own work, is the way Queer Nation, in miming "the privileges of normality" affixes a "camp inflection" onto the "national" (1993, 196). By parodying the symbolic designs of nationalism, Queer Nation undermines the basis on which such a hegemonic institution claims authority. One example of Queer Nation's satire is the "I Hate Straights" campaign that took place during gay pride parades in New York and Chicago in 1990, which Berlant and Freeman describe as a "monologue, a slave narrative without decorum, a manifesto of rage and its politics. Gone, the assimilationist patience of some gay liberation identity politics; gone, the assertive rationality of the 'homosexual' subject who seeks legitimacy through 'straight' protocols, that 'civilization' has been sighted on the cultural margin" (1993, 200). The campaign plays on the action of infamous groups such as the Westboro Baptist Church who picket while holding signs with slogans such as "God hates fags," among others. This is a satirical reversal of legally sanctioned hate speech, turning the *hetero*normative into the *homo*normative, a deconstruction of the privileged "normal." In their discussion of Queer Nation's program, Berlant and Freeman make clear that, "crucial to a sexually radical movement for social change is the *transgression* of categorical distinctions between sexuality and politics" (1993, 196).[2] Intentional transgression and provocation are at the heart of Queer Nation's program of liberationist politics. Their work is the "victory over limits" that is denied in the Foucauldian formulation of the transgressive act.

Though in nations west of the Old Iron Curtain gay pride parades have become rather staid affairs, in many nations east of that line, including Poland, these events remain highly contested. Indeed, in Poland it remains rather more accurate to call them gay rights marches (*marsz równości*) as they are rarely the jubilant, celebratory occasions such parades have become in the United States. One of the earliest marches, taking place in 2004—late by American standards—is immortalized on the cover of the book *Homophobia in Polish* (*Homofobia po polsku*) from 2004. Instead of depicting the *legal* "March of Tolerance" (*Marsz Tolerancji*) that took place in Kraków that same year, the photograph shows an illegal parade of protestors marching in opposition to it. The pictured protestors, who probably outnumbered the participants in the parade, are not dressed in neo-fascist regalia, nor are they skin-heads. They look to be the representatives of Polish "normalcy," and they carry banners reading "Homosexuals of all nations, heal yourselves!" (*Homosexy wszystkich krajów, leczcie się!*), and "Let's kick the homosexuals out of Kraków" (*Wykopmy homoseksów z Krakowa*). While this counter-protest was the illegal one, in the context of Poland it was obviously non-transgressive, whereas the *legal* March of Tolerance was the more transgressive event of the two. In her contribution to the book, Iwona Stefańczyk calls this a "legitimate discrimination" (*słuszna dyskryminacja*)

(2004, 175); it is a discrimination absolutely tolerated and sanctioned by the government.

A later march in 2010, also in Kraków, was captured on video and uploaded to YouTube with the title "Sad gay pride in Kraków." The American vlogger who shot the march notes that the protestors are "surrounded by cops" in riot gear, ostensibly to provide them with protection. What strikes the vlogger as odd is the fact that there seem to be "more police than gay protestors."[3] Watching the video one cannot help but notice the stark contrast between this march and gay pride parades as they have come to look in the United States and Western Europe. There is no music, cheering, nor waving coming from the rather bemused onlookers. The march slowly drags itself through the streets, led by two police vans, and a cordon of riot gear–clad police completely surrounding it. It is difficult for one to discern whether the police are protecting the marchers from possible attacks, or if they are protecting the public from the site of the parade.

One final example comes from a video of a gay rights march in Kraków from 2013, uploaded by Ruptly TV. It is headed by the title "Poland: gay pride starts with a kiss and ends with violence." The video begins with a shot of two men in the parade openly kissing. Though not at all out of the ordinary in the context of the parade, in the wider context of Poland and many Poles' probable reactions to such displays of "homoerotic" affection, one cannot help but feel their kiss as almost the committing of a crime. Surprisingly, the parade takes on an actual celebratory aspect unlike the previous examples, with music, chanting, and a sizable crowd marching through the city. Of course, once again the police surround the marchers in full riot gear, but it finally seems as though they are there to protect the participants instead of to block the view of the parade. After showing various scenes from the event, the video ends as the title suggests—in violence. In the video's description it is noted that while the gay pride parade was taking place, a second march was underway, this one led by "hundreds of impassioned right-wing nationalists gathered in Kraków at the same time to march down the streets in a *Pro-Healthy Family* march."[4] While the second anti-gay pride march was legal, the participants of this "Pro-Healthy Family" contingent clashed repeatedly with the pride parade and with police, throwing bottles and smoke flares. Though the police did protect the pride marchers, and even chased off the nationalist groups, that their march was even allowed to go on at the exact same time as the parade reveals the level of resentment still held against the expression of non-normative identities in Poland. The fact remains that a nationalist, anti-gay march had been sanctioned by the government, and hundreds participated in it. It illustrates that the gay rights parade in Poland, though now legal, remains a socially transgressive act, an important site of subverting the symbolic dominance of heteronormative authority.

While my project reads transgression much more politically than Foucault's theories would seem to allow, one aspect of his thought that I find productive in my own argument is the idea of transgression as a site of identity creation. In discussing the play between the limit and its transgression Foucault states that they "depend on each other for whatever density of being they possess: a limit could not exist if it were absolutely uncrossable and, reciprocally, transgression would be pointless if it merely crossed a limit composed of illusions and shadows" (1977, 34). In short, identification is an oppositional process, revealing that one is only what one is not. Identity is always created in opposition to an Other: the straight person is only straight because they are not gay, and the Pole is only a Pole because they are not a German, Czech, Russian, or Jew. Several scholars have expanded on this idea of transgression as a site of identity formation. Peter Stallybrass and Allon White note that "cultural identity is inseparable from limits, it is always a boundary phenomenon and its order is always constructed around the figures of its territorial edge" (200). This edge or limit describes an inside and an outside that are always present in the configuration of identities. Diana Fuss writes the following in reference to the hetero versus homo oppositional process of identification:

> To the extent that the denotation of any term is always dependent on what is exterior to it [. . .], the inside/outside polarity is an indispensable model for helping us to understand the complicated workings of semiosis. Inside/outside functions as the very figure for signification and the mechanisms of meaning production. It has everything to do with the structures of alienation, splitting, and identification which together produce a self and an other, a subject and an object, an unconscious and a conscious, an interiority and an exteriority. Indeed, one of the fundamental insights of Lacanian psychoanalysis, [. . .] is the notion that any identity is founded relationally, constituted in reference to an exterior or outside that defines the subject's own interior boundaries and corporeal surfaces. (1991, 1–2)

A subject only exists in opposition to another "outside" subject, which in itself reveals the arbitrary, insecure ground on which identities are founded in the first place. For Julian Wolfreys it is the transgression of this line between the inside/outside that "indicates a moment of becoming" (2008, 15). According to Wolfreys, along with it being the "breaking of a code, a rebellion against normative social or cultural constraints," transgression is also "the very pulse that constitutes our identities, and we would have no sense of our own subjectivity were it not for a constant, if discontinuous negotiation with the transgressive otherness by which we are formed and informed" (1). The limit is the axiom by which "members or potential members of whatever the institution in question can measure the extent to which they belong, how they might belong, to what extent they are excluded or can never belong" (4). The limit demands the excluded Other haunting the border, and transgressing that border is central to identity formation.

Later in her introduction, Fuss offers a warning against leaving the hetero/homo hierarchy un-deconstructed: "Homosexuality, read as a transgression against heterosexuality, succeeds not in undermining the authoritative position of heterosexuality so much as reconfirming heterosexuality's centrality precisely as that which must be resisted" (6). Her warning is well taken. It is not enough simply to suggest the transgressivity of non-normative identities, which would do little more than re-entrench the normative as the center, or the "correct" side of the limit. This would fit precisely into Foucault's notion of the "neutrality" of transgression, as neither revolutionary nor conservative. Fuss asserts the possibility of deconstructing such hierarchical oppositions. "That [they] always *tend toward* reestablishing themselves does not mean that they can never be invaded, interfered with, and critically impaired. What it does mean is that we must be vigilant in working against such a tendency: what is called for is nothing less than an insistent and intrepid disorganization of the very structures which produce this inescapable logic" (6). To avoid this tendency toward reestablishing the normative as the privileged center, I begin from the position that transgression is a politically resistant act and not a neutral "accident." In the case of the hetero/homo hierarchy then, the homo is not simply a "sin," an offense against that which is "correct;" rather it actively subverts normativity, revealing its "correctness" as based on a privilege won through a contentious history of compulsory heterosexuality. In their introductory chapter "Sexual Transgression, Social Order and the Self" from the collection *Transgressive Sex: Subversion and Control in Erotic Encounters*, Hastings Donnan and Fiona Magowan misread, I believe, Fuss's warning, and illustrate a rather reactionary understanding of it. They suggest that "a proliferation of transgressive acts can, in fact, lead to a reversal of openness and, despite ongoing access to transgressive possibilities, people and governments may push for policies to control sexual practices either because of pressures upon how they are perceived or because of deleterious effects of sexual transgression upon society" (2009, 22). While it may be true that some "people and governments" might be made uncomfortable by the "deleterious effects" of the non-normative, the proper starting point of inquiry should not be the concern of governments, who are far too invested in the maintenance of normative hegemony, but rather a critical investigation of why that anxiety with "sexual transgression" exists among a community in the first place. It seems that here the use of the term "sexual transgression" is precisely the re-confirmation of "heterosexuality's centrality" against which Fuss warned.

It is my hope the present work can function as one of these "acts of interference" within the Polish political reality for which Fuss calls. By intervening in both the cultural and political life of Poland, I wish to challenge the sometimes subtle but more often open support for nationalist and homophobic voices in Poland. This may be a rather ambitious goal for a work of literary scholarship, but a completely achievable one nonetheless.[5] This, of course, will be a much more achievable goal once this work is translated into Polish. Happily, there has recently been an increasing amount of scholarship within the Polish academy on subjects such as Queer theory, feminism, and nationalism studies. Quite often this is work carried out in American and British studies departments in Polish universities. Three of the most active scholars in the field have been Tomasz Basiuk, Tomasz Sikora, and Dominika Ferens, who have edited several volumes of collected essays. This includes titles such as *Odmiany Odmieńca: Mniejszościowe Orientacje Seksualne W Perspektywie Gender* (*A Queer Mixture: Gender Perspectives on Minority Sexual Identities*, 2002), *Out Here: Local and International Perspectives in Queer Studies* (2006a), and *The Parameters of Desire: The Culture of Queers in the Face of Homophobia* (2006b). This scholarship has gained an impressive foothold in the Polish academy, but the one area that remains rather lacking is the use of these theoretical approaches in an analysis of Polish literature. There have been some more recent exceptions, such as Krzystof Tomasik's *Homobiographies: Polish Writers of the 19th and 20th Century* (2008), as well as his newest book *Gay.R.L: Sexual Minorities in the PRL* (2012). Though both of these works make important interventions into the analysis of several Polish authors in the context of how their sexuality informs their writing, neither provide any real literary analysis, but rather act as literary biographies of Polish authors. There has also been the recent *Literature and Homosexuality: An Introduction to the Issue of Gender in Canonical Texts of World and Polish Literature* (2012) by Ewa Chudoba. Again, while this is certainly a worthwhile intervention in its own right, it stops short of a deep critical analysis, spending less than one hundred pages on Polish literature, and again functioning more as literary biography. Two authors whose works more clearly link the cultural study of gender to an analysis of literature are Błażej Warkocki and Tomasz Kaliściak. Warkocki's book, *Homo niewiadomo* (*The Indeterminate Man*, 2007), makes use of queer theory's insights on identity formation to analyze newer works of the Polish canon, such as Grzegorz Musiał, Andrzej Stasiuk, and Izabela Filipiak. In *Płeć pantofla* (*The Gender of the Slipper*, 2016)[6] Kaliściak traces the ways masculinity was defined and re-defined over the course of the nineteenth and twentieth centuries. He provides excellent analyses of several authors as well-known as Gombrowicz and as obscure as Ludwik Sztyrmer.

To achieve my interference of Polish heteronormativity I analyze several works of twentieth-century Polish fiction transgressively, meaning I read the texts against the grain of a heteronormative ideology that would ignore their queer elements. Through textual explication I investigate the convergence between national and gender identities, particularly in works that transgress traditional nationalist and heteronormative notions of subjectivity, and I analyze how those transgressions subvert such regimes. In reading these works I challenge the many binaries on which reactionary ideology depends in order to maintain its cultural hegemony. As inspiration I look to Julian Wolfreys's notion of "reading transgression":

> It [reading transgression] involves a reorientation of the act of reading, so that reading, responding to those codes or traces that gesture beyond narrative or representational coherence and which exceed the limits of the form, becomes itself transgressive. More specifically, the transgressive reading is one that recognizes those traces in any text which are themselves disruptive of conventional and institutional codes. [. . .] The emphasis on recognition points to what is embedded within the text, reversal then stressing the reader's active work in the production of the text, thereby transgressing the limits of reading after coherence. (12)

Like Wolfreys, my work seeks to "recognize the disruptions" of institutional codes. Specifically, through my counter-discursive readings I will look at the ways in which these texts disrupt the heteronormative codes of gender and nation, exceeding the limits placed on them by conservative Polish ideology. Admittedly, my transgressive reading is not as acrobatic as Wolfreys's. He searches for "traces of disruption" in texts that at first reading do not seem obviously transgressive, such as Spenser's "The Faerie Queene" and the works of Dryden. My project, on the other hand, reads transgression in texts that often quite openly challenge the Catholic-centric nationalism found in Polish culture. For the most part the subject matter of the texts leaves me few traces to discover in terms of their subversive character. In my opinion, however, this does not diminish their revolutionary potential. In the Polish context it is often necessary to write quite bluntly about the topic if one's point is to be made at all clear to the audience. There were a few cases, such as Julian Stryjkowski's novel *In the Willows. . .our Fiddles* in chapter 3 when I was required to do a much more subtle reading in order to reveal the transgressive traces within the text.

The contributors of the quite recent *Being Poland: A New History of Polish Literature and Culture since 1918* (2018) provide further support for these ideas on the importance of transgression in liberationist cultural studies. This voluminous tome provides reinterpretations of important Polish literary movements—beginning with the Baroque cultural formation of Sarmatism, through to twenty-first-century Polish pop culture—and innumerable texts from each of these eras. In part II of the book, various authors propose four "Strategies" to follow in this reinterpretation of Polish culture. For my purposes here, the two most important are the *emancipatory* and *transgressive* strategies. The emancipatory strategy looks to overcome "old norms" and replace them with new ones, "positing its function as liberating and socially progressive" (Trojanowska 2018, xix). The transgressive strategy challenges the rules for deciding the canon, and "seeks out the hidden places, gaps, fissures, and ruptures that allow chaos through" (xix).

In her chapter on the emancipatory strategy, Grażyna Borkowska argues that "the literary 'coming out' of gays and lesbians constitutes a missing element" in the process "of disarming the patriotic and martyrological image of Polish history and culture." It is also central to the modernization of Polish society, "and the fostering of tolerance and of respect for fundamental rights" (qtd. in Trojanowska 2018, 183). For Borkowska, then, the study of gay characters in Polish literature can initiate a progressive interrogation of Polish nationalist culture, and play a part in a liberationist program. The transgressive strategy works hand in glove with the emancipatory. In replacing old norms with new, emancipation depends on transgression to determine what these "new norms" are. As Tamara Trojanowska notes, transgression "challenges, and redraws the limits of the prohibited. [. . .] It traverses value judgments, respect, desire, fear, and disgust" (186). The power of the transgressive lies in its ability to disturb the borderlines, making room for emancipation.

GENDER AND NATION

The philosophical and critical scholarship already done on revealing the constructedness of identity is extensive. As I mentioned at the beginning of this introduction, within academia the idea is nearly axiomatic; however, a short reiteration may be welcomed. Instead of accepting the notion that identity is an always already bounded, stable structure, closer investigation reveals its actual permeability, and therefore instability. Judith Butler theorizes gender identity as a "free floating artifice." In her essay "Imitation and Gender Subordination" she reveals the arbitrary means by which received ideas of a stable gender came to be taken as "natural" or "eternal."

> Although compulsory heterosexuality often presumes that there is first a sex that is expressed through a gender and then through a sexuality, it may now be necessary fully to invert and displace that operation of thought. If a regime of sexuality mandates a compulsory performance of sex, then it may be only through that performance that the binary system of gender and the binary system of sex come to have intelligibility at all. It may be that the very categories of sex, of sexual identity, of gender are produced or maintained in the *effects* of this compulsory performance, effects which are disingenuously renamed as causes, origins, disingenuously lined up within a causal or expressive sequence that the heterosexual norm produces to legitimate itself as the origin of all sex. (1991, 29)

Butler views identity as only a product of the hegemony of compulsory heterosexuality, which demands one "perform" according to the prescripts of an acceptable gender norm. If this is the case, then the originary nature of gender identity is little more than mythology. As a performance, gender is never a stable mode of identification; it is capable of constant change, forever in a state of "becoming" rather than "being." Butler expands on the performativity of gender in her classic *Gender Trouble*. Here she suggests that "sex does not limit gender," and therefore there are "ways of culturally interpreting the sexed body that are in no way restricted by the apparent duality of sex" (1990, 112). In the previously mentioned essay "Inside/Out," Diana Fuss furthers this analysis of the instability of gender identities, noting their reliance on an oppositional mode of definition:

> To protect against the recognition of the lack within the self, the self erects and defends its borders against an other which is made to represent or to become the selfsame lack. But borders are notoriously unstable, and sexual identities rarely secure. Heterosexuality can never fully ignore the close proximity of its terrifying (homo)sexual other, any more than homosexuality can entirely escape the equally insistent social pressures of (hetero)sexual conformity. (3)

The normalcy, or centrality of heterosexuality is forever "haunted" by the necessary presence of homosexuality—necessary because it is only through the *presence* of homosexuality that heterosexuality has any meaning.

Closer scrutiny also reveals the unstable nature of national identity, analogous to that of gender identity. One of the earliest theoretical studies to challenge the traditional view of an immutable nation is Benedict Anderson's *Imagined Communities*. He sees the nation as

> an imagined political community—and imagined as both inherently limited and sovereign. It is *imagined* because the members of even the smallest nation will never know most of their fellow-members, meet them, or even hear of them, yet in the minds of each lives the image of their communion. [. . .] [A]ll communities larger than primordial villages of face-to-face contact (and perhaps even these) are imagined. Communities are to be distinguished, not by their falsity/genuineness, but by the style in which they are imagined. (1983, 6)

Anderson is highly suspicious of any claim to a monolithic commonality between individuals within a group. The nation is not an eternal, homogenous order. Despite nationalist fantasies to the contrary, the nation is elastic and heterogeneous. Any perceived national identity is merely constructed through a nation's politics, history, literature, and cultural discourses.[7] Expanding on Anderson's ideas, Homi Bhabha sees the nation as "an impossible unity"; however, despite this impossibility, national discourses continually attempt "to produce the idea of the nation as a continuous narrative of national progress" (1994, 1). The narrative, or mythology that nationalism creates is that the nation is a bounded unity that always has been and always will be. In order for the nation to be a stable unity, it must always already exist in the nationalist imagination. Joep Leerssen advances these ideas in his work *National Thought in Europe*, stating that the nation, "that thing which is at the core and at the basis of the ideology of nationalism, is a slippery and elusive concept" (2006, 16). He adopts "ethnie" as a more focused term in place of "nation," an "ethnicity" being a group bonded "by a chosen common self-identification. [. . .] This notion of ethnicity emphasizes that what matters in group identity is not any objective presence of real physical or cultural similarities or differences, but rather a group's acknowledgement of perceived similarities or differences, and the willingness to consider them meaningful" (16). For Leerssen, the basis of intersubjective group identification is not the existence of shared *a priori* "biology" or "bloodlines." Instead, it relies on an almost conscious agreement between individuals on a "shared self-image."

For me what truly becomes productive and much more intriguing are the intersections between gender and national identity creation and maintenance. In his discussion of group identity Leerssen continues in a similar vein to Fuss's analysis of the "oppositional" character of gender identity. He sees that such a subjective community as the ethnie "is not in the first instance merely a sense of 'belonging together' as that it involves a sense of being *distinct from others*. In other words, a perceived collective identity, or a shared self-image, presupposes a perceived separation from others, a process of exclusion" (17). Any sense of "collective togetherness" necessarily demands a sense of "collective separateness" (17). In their introduction to the earlier volume *Nationalisms and Sexualities*, the editors also discuss this oppositional quality of national identity, noting that like gender,

> nationality is a relational term whose identity derives from its inherence in a system of differences. In the same way that "man" and "woman" define themselves reciprocally (though never symmetrically), national identity is determined not on the basis of its own intrinsic properties but as a function of what it (presumably) is not. [. . .] But the very fact that such identities depend constitutively on difference means that nations are forever haunted by their various definitional others. (Parker et al. 1992, 5)

More than the parallel processes of their creation, what links gender and nationality much closer to one another is the nationalist desire for an immutable, uniform standard of identity. Joanna Mizielinska notes that the Other in opposition to which the nation is constructed "can be external, i.e. other nations, or the Other can live within the nation, somewhere on the margins, the internal or inner Other" (2001, 283). Because a nation needs to exist in the unity of common identity, "Nationalism invents or constructs identity, basing it on the assumption of the nation's homogeneity" (282). This homogeneity, however, is continually subverted by the existence of various minorities, whether ethnic, religious, or sexual. Tomasz Sikora elaborates on this idea, calling the nation an "effective amalgam of wildly heterogeneous elements soldered up at a discursive level that emphasizes an overall unity" (2004, 65). For nationalist discourse there is a "longing for national coherence, the illusion of which is only possible due to forgetting, excluding, repressing and regulating" (65). Maintaining a stable, impermeable gender identity is one area of such regulation. As Sikora goes on to note, "The discursive construction of nation is replete with heterosexist assumptions and fantasies" (67). Ignoring and even repressing non-normative sexualities is one of the cornerstones of modern nation building. For the illusion of national stability to be maintained, there must be a reproduction of the means of reproduction. Not only are same-sex relationships unproductive, they symbolically become

> active agent[s] of waste, death and destruction—a threat, indeed to civilization itself. [. . .] If in the classical nationalist discourses the *raison d'être* of a nation is procreation [. . .] and defense of its borders, then homosexual activity must be perceived as an unpardonable waste associated with death—but not the heroic death of a soldier sacrificing his life for the nation, but the death of the nation itself [. . .]. In a perfect nation queers ideally do not exist, or if they do they are represented as a threat to the moral integrity, if not the physical health, of the nation. (75)

Classical nationalism, and more specifically Polish nationalism, is necessarily a heteronormative system. It is a regulatory regime with an "insatiable need to administer difference through violent acts of segregation, censorship, economic coercion, physical torture, police brutality" (Parker et. al. 1992, 5). Above all else the nation's "borders," whether political or sexual, must be guarded against invasions and pollution.

> If the body is synecdochal for the social system *per se* or a site in which open systems converge, then any kind of unregulated permeability constitutes a site of pollution and endangerment. Since anal and oral sex among men clearly establishes certain kinds of bodily permeabilities unsanctioned by the hegemonic order, male homosexuality would, within such a hegemonic point of view, constitute a site of danger and pollution. (Butler 1990, 132)

In the Polish nationalist imagination, the penetrated, "polluted" male body is analogous to the invaded national border; both are sites of unforgivable incursion. Neither are of any use to the heteronormative regime of the nation. Ironically, while the permeability of the gay male body is a site of waste, it is the impermeability of the gay female body that is also seen as wasteful for the nation.[8] Both become focuses of nationalist violence; the "open" bodies of gay men are targeted in order to "cleanse" their polluting effects, while gay women and their "closed" bodies are raped in order to force their "productivity" for the nation.[9]

Of course, one must recognize the fact that nationalist ideology is always in flux and subject to change. In the groundbreaking 2007—and recently updated as of 2017—book *Terrorist Assemblages*, Jasbir Puar makes several astute observations about the recent phenomenon of "homonationalism" in the West. Nationalisms of the United States and Western European countries have been quite successful in coopting the concerns of LGBTQ+ communities in order to strengthen their own xenophobia and racism, specifically against the Muslim world. The U.S. war on terror has shifted the "terms of degeneracy" to such a degree that "homosexuality is no longer a priori excluded from nationalist formations" (Puar 2017, 2). While I largely agree with Puar's insights, the fact remains that the situation at this current moment in Poland is quite dissimilar to that in the United States or Western Europe. Nationalists in Poland have not found it necessary to make any gestures toward the LGBTQ+ community that would suggest they have been accepted as full participants in the nation, a fact made immediately clear by both the continued ban on same-sex marriage as well as adoption by same-sex couples (Plucinska 2018). This is why I am careful in this study to refer to either "classical" or "Polish" nationalism specifically.

The roots of modern Polish nationalism, as is the case for many other nationalisms, can be traced to the eighteenth century. What is particular in the Polish example is the fact of the ideology's birth at a time when the nation as such did not exist. After the three partitions of 1772, 1793, and 1795 Poland no longer appeared on any map, being divided between Russia, Prussia, and Austro-Hungary. Except for a brief period from 1815 to 1831 when the pseudo-colonial Congress Kingdom, created by Tsar Alexander, brought Poland back in a nominal form, the "*Rzeczpospolita*" (Res Publica) would remain a non-place until the end of the First World War.[10]

Polish nationalism as a distinct ideology from other nationalisms began to materialize as an integral component of Polish Romanticism. While Romanticism in Poland was influenced by western literary trends, it differed significantly from them in terms of theme and purpose. Whereas Western Romanticism looked inward, into the individual, Polish Romanticism primarily looked for its inspiration to "the heroic fight for national independence and the messianic role ascribed to Poland in its suffering [. . .]. Unabashedly patriotic and spiritual, Polish Romantic poetry held the promise of national resurrection and universal justice" (Mikoś 2002, 8). According to the Romantics, the greatest possible achievement for the individual was his sacrifice in service to the rebirth of the nation. Under the guidance of the triumvirate of Adam Mickiewicz, Julian Słowacki, and Zygmunt Krasiński, a messianic image of Poland came to hold sway. As Geneviève Zubrzycki notes, "the narrative was forcefully created in the nineteenth century by Romantic poets who equated the Partitions of Poland with its crucifixion. Poland, in these writings, was the Christ of Nations: sacrificed for the sins of the world, it would be brought back to life to save humanity" (2007, 119). This masochistic and vampiric ideology would lead to the disasters of three failed uprisings—the November Uprising of 1830, the Greater Poland Uprising of 1848, and the January Uprising of 1863—and the deaths, exile, or imprisonment of much of Poland's cultural and intellectual leadership, including Mickiewicz, Słowacki, and Krasiński, who all died in foreign lands.

The messianism of Polish Romanticism would also have the effect of forever linking Polish national identity to Roman Catholicism. The work of Roman Dmowski (1864–1939), the man widely considered to be "the father of modern Polish nationalism" (Zubrzycki 2006, 53), is most responsible for codifying this connection between the Polish and the Catholic. Dmowski founded the far-right National Democracy party, popularly referred to as "Endecja" in 1897. In 1927 he wrote the following about what he saw as the integral role Catholicism plays in Polish national identification:

> Catholicism is not an appendage to Polishness, coloring it in some way; it is, rather, inherent to its being, in large measure it constitutes its very essence. To attempt to dissociate Catholicism from Polishness, and to separate the nation from its religion and the Church, is to destroy the very essence of the nation. (qtd. in Zubrzycki 2006, 57)

Dmowski believed that being a Pole necessarily meant being a Catholic, a sentiment succinctly expressed in the appellation "*Polak-Katolik*," which he coined. For him the "Pole" side of the term is meaningless in the absence of the "Catholic" side. This ignores and suppresses the existence of religious minorities, including Jews, orthodox Ukrainians, and protestant Germans who made up almost forty percent of the population at the time. In the "*Polak-Katolik*" equation, it is impossible for these groups to partake in the nation-state.

This articulation of the tight "Polish/Catholic" nexus of course is not the soul creation of Dmowski. He was expressing a position that was shared by many at the time. Maria Konopnicka (1842–1910) for example wrote the (in)famous poem "Rota" ("The Pledge") in 1907.[11] It was so popular it was considered for acceptance as Poland's national anthem for a time, and after 1989 even became the anthem for the center-right Polish Peoples' Party. Little is needed in the way of close reading to understand the strong nationalist sentiments expressed in the following two stanzas:

> The German will not spit in our face,
> Nor Germanize our children,
> Our host will arise in arms,

> The Holy Spirit will lead us.
> We will go where the golden horn sounds.
> So help us God!
> So help us God!
> We will not allow Poland's name to be defamed,
> We will not step alive into coffins.
> For Poland's name, for its honor
> We lift our proud heads,
> The grandson will regain his grandfathers' land. (32)

While this is certainly an explicit example of nationalist rhetoric, it is important to keep in mind that the poem was written as a protest against the Prussian occupation of Western Poland and the *Kulturkampf* program. The German Other was a powerful colonizing force, capable of wiping out any future Polish identity through the "Germanization" of Polish children. The greatest defense against this is Catholicism, expressed by the poem's call for "the Holy Spirit" to lead the nation. The restitution of the state is a religious calling, marked by the oath "So help us God!" In the end it is also an entirely masculine project as the final goal is the maintenance of the traditional male to male system of property inheritance as "grand*sons*" will regain the "grand*fathers*'" land, ignoring the existence of women as participants in the nation. This is perhaps the most surprising element of the poem as Konopnicka was an early feminist, heavily involved in women's rights activism.

One final example of nationalist expression from the time is the poem, "Catechism of the Polish Child" written in 1900 by Władysław Bełza (1847–1913).

> Who are you?
> A little Pole.
> What's your symbol?
> The white eagle.
> Where do you live?
> Among my own.
> In what nation?
> In the Polish land.
> What is this land?
> My Fatherland.
> By what was it won?
> With blood and scar.
> [...]
> What are you for her?
> A grateful child.
> What do you owe her?
> To give my life.

The poem's assertion of the interconnection between Catholicism and Polishness begins with the very title. The choice of the catechism form reveals the national project to be a religious undertaking. When asked "In what do you believe?" the child answers "I believe in Poland." But belief is a religious expression of faith. The nation and the church have become one and the same. An essential role of the nationalist project is the indoctrination of the young. The "little Pole" must be willing to sacrifice himself, to give his life for the good of the nation, which takes on a vampiric quality as it demands this through "blood and scar." Interestingly, when asked "Where do you live," the child does not respond "in Poland," but rather, "among my own." In the absence of the political institution of Poland, the nation must rely on its expression through the very bodies of Poles, meaning that group of individuals who have agreed on a common self-image.

In more recent history Polish nationalist expression has continued along a similar trajectory. There are several nationalist groups active within the country.[12] While all of them are undeniably involved in racist, anti-Semitic, and anti-immigrant activities, there are two points common in all of their official programs: the desire to strengthen the influence of the Catholic Church in state politics, and virulent opposition to gay rights. The National Rebirth of Poland group (NOP) was featured in a short documentary film "Pretty Radical" by *The Guardian* about the increasing presence of young women in nationalist groups. The National Radical Camp (ONR) has held marches commemorating the 1936 anti-Jewish riots in the town of Myślenice. The Association for Tradition and Culture or "Niklot," named after a twelfth-century pagan Slavic prince, promotes a form of ethnic nationalism. The All-Polish Youth has been singled out by Amnesty International for their homophobia and racist actions. Probably the most successful nationalist group in the last few decades has been the League of Polish Families (LPR). In 2001 they won almost 8 percent of the vote, giving them thirty-eight seats in the Polish Sejm. Though certainly a small proportion of the representation, they had a large enough showing to win them a junior partnership when Law and Justice (PiS) formed a government. Happily, this would not last long, and in 2007 LPR failed to reach the 5 percent ceiling needed to hold seats in the Sejm. During his tenure as Education Minister, the party's leader, Roman Giertych—whose family has had close ties to nationalist groups going back to Roman Dmowski—attempted to remove the works of Witold Gombrowicz—whose work I analyze in the first chapter—from the national secondary school curriculum. All of these groups have relationships with the Catholic National Movement (RKN). If one visits their website ojczyzna.pl (fatherland) one is immediately presented with an image of the crucified Christ along with the following declaration:

> Christ was murdered on the cross for teaching love, good, and the truth. Our entire national, and European history and tradition is based on His teachings. This is known by every honest person, though he may not be a believer. Attacks on the symbol of Christ are only committed by those who are deprived of all moral and ethical principles: BARBARIANS.

This passage unequivocally equates Christianity with European civilization, which ultimately seems to be the only civilization. Those who do not admit Christ's teachings as fundamental to the European (civilized) identity are the uncivilized. Further down the page the RKN makes their vision of "true" Polishness clearer: "Catholic Poland still has not died." This is an overt play on the first line from the Polish national anthem: "Poland still has not died" (*Jeszcze Polska nie zginęła*). Again, what becomes obvious is the desire of Polish nationalists to make the "Pole" meaningless in the absence of the "Catholic." Within the configuration of the "*Polak-Katolik*" the "*Polak-Gej*" is an impossibility. Just one example of the centrality of homophobia to Polish nationalist ideology is the several recent burnings of the Warsaw Rainbow. This is a sculpture of a rainbow by award-winning artist Julita Wójcik placed in Warsaw's Savior Square in 2012 (Kozlowska, 2013). According to Wójcik it was meant as an apolitical symbol of hope. However, over the past few years the sculpture has been damaged or burned down several times by right-wing groups believing it to be a symbol of gay rights.

Fortunately, there have been rising counter-narratives in Poland to this virulent nationalism, symbolized by the rebuilding of the Warsaw Rainbow after every destructive event. Several LGBTQ+ rights groups have emerged over the past several years.[13] Lambda Warsaw was founded in 1997, making it the oldest operating gay rights association in Poland. It has organized HIV/AIDS prevention programs, as well as anti-discriminatory events. Not The Same, founded in 2001, is a Queer studies group based in Wrocław University. It organizes lectures and conferences for students and scholars. The Campaign Against Homophobia (KPH) was also founded in 2001. It has organized several anti-homophobic campaigns, including the now famous "Let Them See Us" installation. This was a series of photographs of gay and lesbian couples holding hands in the streets of Polish cities that were then posted onto billboards throughout Poland. Though advertising companies bowed to pressure and took the billboards down, the campaign was hugely successful in instigating a discussion about gay rights in Poland. Perhaps the most inspiring development in the last few years in the fight for equal rights for the LGBTQ+ community is the election to the Sejm in 2011 of not only Poland's first openly gay man, Robert Biedroń, but the country's first (and the world's only) openly transgender person, Anna Grodzka ("Poland Swears in First Transsexual" 2011). Biedroń would later become Poland's first openly gay mayor, elected to the position in 2014 in the city of Słupsk ("Poland

Elects its First Openly Gay Mayor" 2015). While these are certainly major successes in the struggle for more acceptance of non-normative identities in Poland, the progressive minded should remain vigilant in the face of the continued presence and activity of far-right organizations.

A NOTE ON AUTOFICTION

Most of the texts I analyze in the following work conform to the genre known as "autofiction." The term was first coined in 1977 by Serge Doubrovsky in his novel *Fils* (*Threads/Son*), seeing it as "a genre between fiction and autobiography" that would "blend traditional notions of fiction and reality" (McDonough 2011, 7–9). It differs from autobiography in that it does not seek to recount point by point the factual events of the author's life. In a sense, it is the literary fictionalization of an author's autobiography. In her analysis of *Fils*, Sarah McDonough notes that it "reflects not only what happened in Doubrovsky's life, but also his psychological perception of those events" (17), moving beyond the simple retelling of his life. According to Anna Turczyn, autofiction is "the determination of the autobiographical 'I' as a linguistic entity, which occurs outside of real time and space, and which determines its existence unconsciously" (2007, 210). It is not the portrayal of a life or "fitting it into a coherent history at the end of which some kind of sense is revealed," but rather it is the "complete sundering of the I, and the undermining of the foundations of the 'certainty of the *self*'" through affixing the identity of the author, the narrator, and the character with the inscription 'novel/fiction'" (205). The ambiguity in defining the line between author and narrator locates autofiction within a postmodern tradition described by uncertainty and instability, refusing the reader solid ontological grounding.

There is little Anglophone scholarship about autofiction. The few pieces that can be found in English are almost exclusively about Francophone literature. This may be in part due to the genre's continental roots. Given the influence French culture has had on the development of Polish culture it is not surprising that autofiction has made its way into Polish literature. In Polish literary scholarship the term "*autofikcja*" is often used with no explanation of its meaning. I found the term used several times by Polish critics discussing many of the works I analyze. Within Polish literary scholarship it seems simply to be an understood designation for a certain genre of short stories and novels that, to a lesser or greater degree, adhere to the aforementioned criteria. One of the clearest examples of autofiction from the texts I analyze is Witold Gombrowicz's 1994 *TransAtlantyk*. From the very beginning of the novel there appears a tension between the fictional and the autobiographical. It opens with Gombrowicz-the-narrator/hero arriving in Buenos Aires days before the German invasion of Poland that would start the Second

World War. This and other moments within the text are taken directly from Gombrowicz-the-author's life as "corroborated" in his also semi-fictionalized *Diaries*. However, the narrative also depicts several surreal moments which obviously could not have taken place in reality. These include the "Parable of the Chevaliers," in which several characters are trapped in a small room for several days jabbing each other with sharpened spurs, as well as the scene of Gonzalo's estate, which depicts, among other impossibilities, the hybrid offspring of dogs and rats. Though such fantastical moments make it clear that *TransAtlantyk* is a work of fiction, it remains impossible for the reader to completely separate Gombrowicz-the-author from Gombrowicz-the-narrator. The line between the two remains ambiguous, creating a narrative genre in the interstices of fiction and autobiography. The use of autofiction in many of the works I analyze makes the line between narrator and author utterly ambiguous, creating a narrative at the interstices of fiction and autobiography. With this in mind, it becomes important in analyzing these stories to avoid falling into the trap of attempting to determine authorial intent: an endeavor both impossible to achieve and, really, quite boring and useless.[14]

THE WORK AT HAND

Though the main consideration in my choice of texts was their transgressive possibilities, what also played a role in my decision was their relative obscurity. Most of the works I analyze have never been translated into English, and of the three that have only *TransAtlantyk* has been studied extensively. Some of the following works even remain largely unknown in Poland. In her book *The Kingdom of Insignificance*, Joanna Niżyńska discusses what she calls the "transatlantic canon"—that is,

> the corpus of literary works that circulates in the North American cultural sphere and is considered by the English-speaking audience to be representative of Polish literature. This canon is subject to political and economic considerations that drive the market for translations, changes in the educational curriculum that render some authors more desirable than others, and, ultimately, a cultural tendency to reinforce rather than challenge the familiar understandings of foreign literatures. (2013, 7)

Undeniably, part of the goal of this project is to present an American audience with works and authors who are largely unknown in the Anglophone world, to expand the transatlantic canon. While some of the novels do have a readership in the West, the specific innovation I provide is my queer reading of them.

In chapter 1, "Iwaszkiewicz and Gombrowicz: Sex, Death, and Panic," I compare Witold Gombrowicz's *TransAtlantyk* (1953 [1994]) and Jarosław Iwaszkiewicz's *Nauczyciel* (*The Teacher*, 1936 [1996]) along the axis of Eve Sedgwick's notion of "homosexual panic," as well as in terms of the play between Eros and Thanatos that appears in the narratives. In both works the homosexual panic experienced by the characters is a product of the enduring influence of Polish Romanticism, especially of its messianic ideology of nationalism. The stories are reflections of one another, both attempting to dismantle the same systems of power. While in *The Teacher* Iwaszkiewicz uses realism to make plain the danger and tragedy inherent in heteronormative and nationalist ideologies, in *TransAtlantyk* Gombrowicz employs a surreal parody to ridicule these same ideologies. Both Iwaszkiewicz and Gombrowicz attempt to subvert heteronormative regimes—Iwaszkiewicz through plain, sober language that reveals the tragedy behind the values of such systems, Gombrowicz through a satire that shows these same values to be ridiculous and laughable.

Chapter 2, "Julian Stryjkowski: The Pole, the Jew, the Queer," traces Julian Stryjkowski's life-long resistance to limitations on his identity. The three works I analyze, *Na Wierzbach . . . Nasze Skrzypce* (*In the Willows . . . Our Fiddles*, 1974), *Tommaso del Cavaliere* (1982), and his final published work of fiction, *Milczenie* (*Silence*, 1993) reveal a rejection of what he sees as the false choice between being Polish and being Jewish, a refusal to see them as mutually exclusive identities. These works illustrate a conviction that for Stryjkowski there is no selection to be made. In each, his struggle with this Polish/Jewish binary is made more complicated by his communism and his queer sexuality.

The next chapter, "Marian Pankowski: The Anti-Martyr," discusses what I see as Marian Pankowski's radical political project in his struggle against the nationalism and martyrology he believed to be deeply imbedded in, and ultimately ruinous of Polish culture. His condemnations of these systems are made through the use of explicit, unabashed queer erotics that subvert all traditional Polish values. He engages in a very clear critical project against outdated modes of national identity creation, which he achieves through sharply parodying Polish provincialism, and satirizing the mythos of Polish suffering.

In chapter 4, "Olga Tokarczuk: Transgressive Bodies, Transgressing Borders," I analyze Tokarczuk's *Silesian Trilogy* from the 1990s: *E.E.* (1995), *Prawiek i inne czasy* (*Longago and Other Times*, 1996), and *Dom dzienny dom nocny* (*House of Day, House of Night*, 1998). In the course of these works Tokarczuk first uses a feminist deconstructive methodology and later a queer post-modern aesthetic in order to subvert notions of stable borders between nations, genders, and ethnicities. In each novel the contested geographical space of Silesia (*Śląsk*) becomes a leitmotif of the fluidity and porous character of such borders. This is an especially important theme in the historical context of the post-socialist 1990s, during which the borders of Central and Eastern Europe once again went through a period of instability and change. Taking into account Tokarczuk's engagement with both feminism and queer theory, her novels become a forum for minority voices that resist heteronormative power structures of nationalism and patriarchy.

I finish the book with a short epilogue that briefly discusses queer liberation in Poland since the beginning of the twenty-first century, finishing on a cautiously optimistic note for the future. More importantly, I use this space for a short discussion of Jerzy Nasierowski's life and work. Although he represents probably the most transgressive figure of this book, due to constraints on time and research possibilities, I was unable to devote an entire chapter to him. I hope to rectify this in the future.

The early Modernist French play *Ubu Roi* from 1896, a scathing satire of political norms and religious morality, describes its setting in the following way: "The action takes place in Poland, that is to say, nowhere."[15] In literal terms, the description is quite apt, considering Poland had not existed on any maps since 1795 following the Third Partition. It bespeaks the deep cultural and political turmoil—as well as identity crisis—Poland had been suffering for over one hundred years. Although Poland is no longer nowhere, for our current purposes the sentiment is a potent metaphor, describing a borderlessness that characterizes identities and political geographies despite the fantasies of structure and coherence held by regimes invested in the unitary nation state.

NOTES

1. All translations from Polish are my own unless otherwise noted.
2. Emphasis added.
3. https://www.youtube.com/watch?v=hy5KaddMawc.
4. https://www.youtube.com/watch?v=Aeqp4KOMJ4A. Emphasis added.
5. In "Imitation and Gender Subordination," Judith Butler expresses a similar conviction about the political potential of scholarship: "If the political task is to show theory is never merely *theoria*, in the sense of disengaged contemplation, and to insist that it is fully political (*phronesis* or even *praxis*), then why not simply call this operation *politics*, or some necessary permutation of it?" (1991, 15).
6. It is important to note that the translation of "pantofel" as "slipper" is literal, and does not express the more obvious use of the term as euphemism for a "hen-pecked husband."
7. For Anderson the major contribution to the invention of the imagining of the nation in eighteenth-century Europe was the rise of print capital, "the novel and the newspaper. For these forms provided the technical means for 're-presenting' the *kind* of imagined community that is the nation" (1983, 25).
8. STDs are another form of "pollution" of the national body. The diseased are often rejected by nationalist ideologies as dangerous to the nation.
9. These kinds of violent reactions to gay people were dramatically exhibited in a recent episode of the HBO documentary series *Vice*, "A Prayer for Uganda." This, of course, is not to

suggest that rape is only used against gay women. The rape of straight women and men is a far too common occurrence, and is often used as a weapon during armed conflicts. However, my concern in this work is the violence perpetrated against queer bodies.

10. See Zamoyski (2009, 218–231).

11. For more on the history of the writing of "Rota" and biographical sketch of Konopnicka see Trochimczyk (2000).

12. For a more thorough presentation of right-wing groups in Poland, see Rafal Pankowski (2006).

13. For a short history of gay rights in Poland, see Baer (2009).

14. For a further discussion of the use of autobiography in fiction see Czermińska (2019).

15. "Quant à l'action qui va commencer, elle se passe en Pologne, c'est-à-dire nulle part."

Chapter One

Iwaszkiewicz and Gombrowicz

Sex, Death, and Panic

My intervention into Polish society's understandings of non-normative identities begins with a comparative analysis of two works from the first half of the twentieth century: *The Teacher*, by Jarosław Iwaszkiewicz, and *TransAtlantyk*, by Witold Gombrowicz. My comparison will make use of Eve Sedgwick's theory of "homosexual panic" in terms of how this panic informs the pieces' erotic and thanatic themes.[1] In both works, characters who represent traditional Polish culture experience homosexual panic, which is revealed as a product of the enduring influence of Polish Romanticism, especially of its messianic ideology of nationalism. Each story also presents other characters whose transgressive sexual practices work to dismantle such normative hegemonical regimes, their transgressions proving to be a productive, subversive force.

Iwaszkiewicz and Gombrowicz are two authors whose works are rarely mentioned together, and indeed they seem to share very little in common that would warrant such a study. Iwaszkiewicz's prose remained thoroughly realist throughout his career, his longest, and most heralded work, the three volume *Fame and Glory* (1956) being a work of historical fiction. Both Gombrowicz's prose and drama, on the other hand, were quite experimental and absurdist, beginning with his novel *Ferdydurke* (1937). Their biographies also seem to work against comparison. While Gombrowicz remained abroad from 1939 until his death in 1969, Iwaszkiewicz stayed in Poland throughout the Second World War and even took part in the communist government after 1945, acting as president of the Polish Writers' Union (*Związek Literatów Polskich*) (Kołakowski 2002, xi). Aside from the fact that they were both Polish, the only other similarity in their biographies seems to be their transgressive sexualities. Iwaszkiewicz's gayness was an "open secret" even during the years of Soviet socialist rule from 1945 until his death in 1980. Krzystof Tomasik notes this in his work *Homobiographies*:

> He didn't at all hide his homosexual tendencies and was one of the first in literature (at least in Poland) who gave it a face in his works. Even strangers knew. And so, when news came that he was marrying the beautiful Miss Lilpopówna—one of the wealthiest young women in Poland—Varsovians who were interested in literature were quite surprised. (2008, 91)

According to Alan Kucharski, "Gombrowicz's confessions of homosexuality—or more precisely bisexuality—from the *Diary* through *A Kind of Testament* [. . .] were accompanied by two works with openly homosexual elements: the novel *TransAtlantyk* [. . .] and the unfinished play *History*" (1998, 267–68). This similarity in their "homobiographies," to use Tomasik's term, then, opens a space for a comparative analysis of their two stories that thematically revolve around queer sexuality and the tension or panic it creates in the nationalist imaginary. The geographic settings of these works are also as distant as the two writers' biographical trajectories. While *The Teacher* takes place in the most Polish of settings, a manor in the eastern "Kresy"[2] of Polish Ukraine, a place highly romanticized throughout Polish literary history, *TransAtlantyk*'s setting is the Polish diaspora of Buenos Ares, Argentina. This geographical difference, however, instead of working against a comparative study of the two, actually enhances such an analysis, especially in terms of how each subverts nationalism and heteronormativity as expressed by Polish culture both at home and abroad.

Eve Sedgwick (1990) develops her ideas on "homosexual panic" in her chapter "The Beast in the Closet," from the book *Epistemology of the Closet*. For Sedgwick this is a panic not experienced by gay men, but instead by heterosexual men. It is a panic heterosexual men experience regarding the possible perception of their homo*social* activities as actually being homo*sexual*. The assurance of a clearly defined and strictly maintained border between the two categories is quite complicated in societies that demand men maintain highly intimate homosocial relationships—such as on sports teams, in the military, or in social clubs. According to Sedgwick these homosocial bonds are a necessary part of maintaining patriarchal hegemony, as they are the means through which men sustain systems of exchange, or what she calls

> the complex web of male power over the production, reproduction, and exchange of goods, persons, and meanings. [. . .] Because the paths of male entitlement [. . .] required certain intense male bonds that were not readily distinguishable from the most reprobate bonds, an endemic and ineradicable state of [. . .] homosexual panic became the normal condition of male heterosexual entitlement. (1990, 185)

The regimes of homosocial relationships uphold strict systems of regulation over their subjects, meting out punishment to those who transgress the line between homo*sociality* and homo*sexuality*—such as the dishonorable discharge from the United States military for breaking the "don't ask don't tell" policy that remained law from the 1990s until 2011. Although Sedgwick deploys her theory of homosexual panic in her discussion of various works of nineteenth-century English fiction, her theory can prove quite productive in an analysis of twentieth-century Polish fiction. In her work, Sedgwick sees homosexual panic as a product of Post-Romanticism in England coming out of what she calls the "paranoid Gothic" genre.[3] In the example of Poland I would suggest homosexual panic is also a product of Romanticism; however, in the Polish example it has much more to do with the messianic, nationalist ideal championed by Polish Romantic authors.

The epic of Polish Romanticism, Adam Mickiewicz's "Pan Tadeusz" (1834 [1992]), provides the model of the ideal Polish man. At the end of the poem, Tadeusz marries Zosia instead of continuing his affair with Telimena, complying with his father's wishes as the marriage ends a generations' long feud between two noble Polish families, which, metaphorically, simultaneously ends the division of the Polish nation since the last Partition. Mickiewicz wishes to illustrate that by submitting to patriarchal authority, order can be maintained, and will ultimately heal the nation. Within this order marriage should be no more than a community-binding social contract. Immediately following the wedding, Tadeusz leaves to join Napoleon's legions in their march to Russia. In his essay "Queering the Heterosexist Fantasy of the Nation," Tomasz Sikora points out the ways in which marriage, in what he terms the "marriage myth," is imagined by nationalist ideology as the "basic social unit" in the establishment of the nation (2004, 67). In this nationalist myth, the very foundations of the nation begin with heterosexual marriage. This ideological imagining has been re-enacted several times throughout the history of Poland. For example, Sikora points to the two times Poland was symbolically "wedded" to the Baltic Sea, once in 1920, by general Jozef Haller, and again in 1945 after the country's liberation from the Germans.[4] An even earlier example is the "crowning" of the Virgin Mary as the eternal queen of Poland in the seventeenth century. These symbolic actions confirm the connection between the maintenance of heterosexual marriage and the solidity of the nation, which Tadeusz reaffirms through his marriage to Zosia. Polish Romanticism was a project centered on the recuperation of the nation. It idealized self-sacrifice for this cause as the highest good. Through his willingness to fight and die for Poland, and to repress his passion, Tadeusz reaffirms the basic elements of the Romantic Polish hero, who puts the good of the nation before all else.

Homosexual panic as manifested in works of Polish literature is a direct result of this Romantic nationalist ideology. In her analysis of subversive bodily acts in *Gender Trouble*, Judith Butler discusses Mary Douglas's idea of the body being a model for any bounded system such as the nation-state (1990, 132). Through the creation and maintenance of compulsory heterosexuality there is an attempt to create an impermeable social system. For heteronormative regimes the male body must be a closed, impenetrable system, which in turn becomes a metaphor for how the nation should also be imagined. For the nation to remain a stable unity, it cannot allow infiltration. The homosexual body, however, is an open, penetrable system. For heteronormativity it becomes a site of infiltration and pollution. This openness then subverts the nationalist ideal of the nation being a closed-off unity, and as Sikora points out, it must be ignored in order for the fantasy of the homogenous nation to continue to exist (65). If the male body is realized as fluid and porous, there is no longer any reason not to realize the nation itself as fluid and porous, as a heterogeneity instead of a homogeneity.

In his book *Eros and Thanatos* (1970), Ryszard Przybylski uses Freud's ideas of the sex and death drives to provide an analysis of Iwaszkiewicz's work through the lens of the relationship between the erotic and thanatic. In his study of Iwaszkiewicz's novella *The Birch Grove* (1933), Przybylski says, "death can only mean something for a life that is conceived as above all else an incessant duration of the organic world. Iwaszkiewicz's certainty that death is the source of life may even have a religious character" (1970, 179). For Przybylski, *The Birch Grove* is a perfect illustration of Iwaszkiewicz's concern with the tension between the sex drive and the death drive which appears in nearly all of his works. Przybylski states, "death and dying are the source of life. [. . .] Such a proposition allows for understanding Staś's soul as a place of battle between the life drive and the death drive, that is [. . .] between Eros and Thanatos. This is why the erotic awakens in Staś the life instinct and makes him deny the death instinct" (189). While I find Przybylski's analysis correct, it is also incomplete in my opinion without an analysis of *The Teacher*. Not only can the point of contact between the erotic and thanatic provide a productive lens for examination of both *The Teacher* and *TransAtlantyk*, it also further develops Sedgwick's ideas on homosexual panic. An intrinsic element in regimes of control is a system of punishment. The panic that queer erotics elicit within heteronormative structures demands disciplinary action. In both works queer desire leads to punishment and death. Ultimately, the queer erotic demands a thanatic response.

THE TEACHER

The Teacher was originally published with another novella, *The Mill on the River Utrata* in 1936. Since that publication very little has been said about it. It is partly due to this silence that I chose to include it here. Though it has been reprinted several times over the years in various collections, there has been little scholarly mention of it. There have been several literary biographies written about Iwaszkiewicz both during his life and after his death in 1980. Within the Polish examples, Janusz Rohozinski's from 1968, Andrzej Gronczewski's from 1972, H.D. Verves's from 1974 (originally written in Ukrainian and translated into Polish), and Andrzej Zawada's from 1994 there was not one mention of *The Teacher*. They all, to some degree, discuss Iwaszkiewicz's literary works, mostly in chronological order, and they all skip over any discussion of *The Teacher*. The first mention of the piece is from a review of the collection by Jan Lorentowicz in the journal *New Book* (Nowa książka) in 1936. Most of the review, which is quite dismissive of the book, is dedicated to the accompanying novella *The Mill on the River Utrata*. What little he does say about *The Teacher* reveals his distaste for the subject matter. In discussing the titular character's secret he says, "this young man, educated, a patriot, an expert on art and literature, having impressed the house with his culture, was a degenerate" (582).[5] Another review of the collection also appeared in 1937, this time in the Journal *Straight from the Bridge* (Prosto z mostu), written by none other than Jerzy Andrzejewski. Again, the piece gives very little space to *The Teacher*, but what little that is said reveals a real tension around the topic of homoeroticism. "In the moment when he realizes that the teacher loves him because of his beauty and because he is a young boy—Felek breaks down. His idealism has been betrayed, and the purity of his feelings has been entangled in the dark circle of inversion" (4). Andrzejewski's description of "the dark circle of inversion," using a term for homosexuality that was all but extinct by 1936, is especially curious given the "open secret" of his own sexuality.[6] Several other reviews of the collection appear throughout the rest of the twentieth century, but they are only interesting in their lack of discussion of *The Teacher*. The first scholarly analysis of any kind of the novella does not appear until 1993 in a short article by Andrzej Selerowicz entitled "Queer: Jarosław Iwaszkiewicz 1894–1980" ("Odmieńcy: Jarosław Iwaszkiewicz 1894–1980"). Though it appears in a journal entitled *Differently: The Writing of Sexual Minorities*, it provides only three sentences to a discussion of *The Teacher*. Granted, the article's topic is Iwaszkiewicz's "homobiography;" however, it strikes one as curious that the piece would not provide a deeper analysis of his arguably most homoerotic work. German Ritz's *Jarosław Iwaszkiewicz: A Border Crosser of the Modern* (1996) is the next scholarly work to discuss *The Teacher*. It is telling that the first time any real critical work on the story was written, it was in German by a Swiss scholar, and not in Polish by a Polish scholar. Even the English translation of *The Birch Grove and Other Stories* from 2002, which is made up of the first several stories from his 1969 *Collected Works* does not include it, though it appears in the original collection before other stories that do make it into the translated collection. Quite recently this trend of silence has begun to change. In her 2012 book *Literature and Homosexuality*, Ewa Chudoba provides a short but insightful analysis of *The Teacher* and its theme of queer desire. The Polish press has also begun mentioning the story in their discussions of Iwaszkiewicz. With my analysis here I hope to add to the scholarly work on *The Teacher*, to bring it a bit more out of the academic closet.

Iwaszkiewicz's story is about a teacher who comes to live with a Polish gentry family to teach the narrator and his two older brothers. This situation actually reflects Iwaszkiewicz's own biography, as he too worked as a live-in teacher for a baron's sons on their estate.[7] The familial situation is one of absent parents, whose children are raised by the help. The father is continually traveling to his various land holdings, returning home for one or two days before leaving again. The mother is a stereotypical bedridden woman who constantly has headaches that force her to remain in her apartments. This rather misogynist description of womanhood, illustrated in other female characters in the story, appears in many of Iwaszkiewicz's works throughout his career.

As soon as he arrives, the teacher shows an affinity toward Felek, the oldest of the three sons. The narrator describes Felek as "being the strongest out of us all, though with his delicate face he was similar to momma. He easily blushed and had beautiful black eyebrows" (193). Within Felek there are both the most masculine and at the same time the most feminine of features; though strong he is also delicate. This mixture of manliness and womanliness will appear again in the character of Ilko, a young Ukrainian farmhand who works on the estate. That the teacher eventually acts on his desire for this "masculine femininity" with Ilko and not Felek illustrates the class tensions that are also at play alongside the sexual tensions within the story.

After the first few lessons the teacher praises Felek to the mother as a wonderful student, which the narrator finds hard to believe as Felek had never been much of a student before. A pattern develops where in the evenings the teacher begins giving impromptu lectures to the household, usually on ancient Greece. At one point the narrator states that the teacher sitting with Felek "was a scene from the Acropolis. He would begin by telling him about Pericles, then about Greek art, and finally about architecture and its orderliness" (196). This Grecian image returns throughout the story. The teacher and Felek develop a classical mentor/student coupling, reminiscent of Socrates and Plato, Plato and Aristotle, Aristotle and Alexander. Often the narrator describes the image of the teacher tutoring Felek as an "idyll," which begins to annoy the narrator as the story continues. This reference to ancient Greece paired with the teacher/student dynamic also brings to mind Plato's *Symposium*, in which Pausanias discusses the sublimity of the love between an older man and a boy who wishes to gain wisdom (1994, 13–19). Ewa

Chudoba reads this relationship similarly, stating, "Their relation constitutes in a way the realization of the Greek *paiderastia*" (2012, 231).

The connection between the erotic and thanatic are always present in the relationship between the teacher and Felek. One of the first important scenes that both strengthens the mutual affection between them and simultaneously illustrates the persistent danger involved in their relationship takes place as the family are returning from a visit with a neighbor and a night of dancing with their daughters. During the ride home in the dark, Felek's horse loses its way and throws him into the snow. The teacher rushes into the darkness and returns carrying Felek to the carriage. The narrator describes how Felek, "pressed himself to Mr. Kazimierz. [. . .] The teacher, holding Felek on his lap, sat next to momma, and thus we drove home" (205). This scene further illustrates Felek's delicateness, while the teacher takes on the more masculine role of protector. The fact that this happens immediately after a disappointing evening in the company of women reinforces the connection between the two. Neither of them had embraced women in dancing earlier, in a house filled with women, but now they embrace each other. Felek is not seriously hurt and his insistence on holding on to the teacher seems due more to his affection for him rather than his injury. It is an embrace that is prompted and excused by peril.

The erotic and thanatic collide in several other scenes throughout the story, and always in an erotic context. One involves a young Frenchman named Romain, who comes to the manor to stay with the family for a short time. He does not seem to fit in with the house, having to stay in little more than a closet and manifesting his boredom with rural life. His outsider status is highlighted even more by the fact that he had been living with the very neighbors whom the family had been visiting in the earlier scene. The teacher takes an interest in Romain, conducting conversations with him in French about literature, which upsets Felek. After going to town with a friend for the evening, Romain returns looking haggard. He then goes to a pharmacy and begins gargling with strong-smelling medicine (207–208). Upon hearing about this, Felek informs the teacher, and Romain is forced to relate the episode to the other men of the house. During the conversation he "quite openly admitted to the bad luck he had encountered, accusing 'Gypsy women,' or as he said 'Jewesses' [. . .] of especially spiteful attributes" (208). The narrator then says that "Mr. Kazimierz laughed with visible constraint, Felek blushed and glanced at him with a pleading, agitated look, and I had no idea whatsoever what was going on" (208). The narrator provides no explicit description of Romain's affliction, only that it was the fault of "spiteful" Jewish women.[8] The adult reader, however, can assume that he believes he has contracted an STD. Taking into account Felek's embarrassment, and the discussion Felek and the narrator have later, he has most likely contracted it through oral sex.

Even though Felek is at first repulsed and embarrassed by Romain's descriptions, after a brief conversation with the teacher he is able to unabashedly discuss the very same issues with his younger brother. The narrator then says of the conversation that it

> was a critical turning point in my life. Obviously, I was already quite aware about things. Since childhood, my mother had made sure of that. But complications from sexual diseases remained alien to me, simply unknown. [. . .] In Felek's outpouring I felt a sudden release, like the breaking of a dam. It seemed that he needed and even wanted to talk at length and in detail about everything that he told me. [. . .] How was it that these things happened in the world? My innocent, beloved world, where animals reproduced calmly and appropriately, as though on a large breeding farm, ceased to exist for me forever, and now everywhere terrible possibilities emerged tangled, obscene, ubiquitous, and dragging behind themselves the complications of sexual relations that had absolutely nothing to do with the procreation of the human species. (208–09)

Since the narrative is related to the reader through the eyes of a twelve-year-old, the references to sex and other "adult" issues are inferred rather than explicitly spelled out. As German Ritz points out, "In *The Teacher*, the nearness of the narrator to the erotic interaction is indeed greater; however, it is neutralized by the prepubescent inexperience of the boy, who recollects the scandal of the homosexual live-in teacher" (1996, 99–100).[9] The young-boy-as-narrator is a perfect narrative device for Iwaszkiewicz to use in reporting the events of the story as he can only report what he understands. This allows Iwaszkiewicz to maintain the ambiguous character of the narrative as well as the silence around non-normative sexuality. As Sedgwick points out in *Epistemology of the Closet*, "the possibility of an embodied male-homosexual thematics has [. . .] a precisely liminal presence. It is present as a [. . .] thematics of absence, and specifically of the absence of speech" (201). Sex and sexuality are described in the silences of the text, which speak further to the ineffability of transgressive sexuality.[10] Therefore, when the narrator first hears about "deviations" in the sexual world, Iwaszkiewicz leaves it unclear to the reader what those deviations might be. Since the narrator later refers to these deviations as having "absolutely nothing to do with the procreation of the human species," it must be inferred that Felek has told him either about oral sex, male to female anal sex, same-sex intercourse, or about all three. Tellingly he describes Felek's explanations as making him feel a kind of "release," "like the breaking of a dam." The narrator has suddenly been opened up, polluted by this new knowledge of "deviant" sexuality.

Though this is not the narrator's introduction into the realm of sex, it is the first time he has learned of sexually transmitted diseases. The erotic and thanatic are immediately interwoven in his consciousness. It is a moment of division reminiscent of a pre- versus post-lapsarian theme. His discussion with Felek is a symbolic eating of the forbidden fruit of the Tree of Knowledge. He is suddenly aware of the sexual body. His "innocent, beloved world" where reproduction takes place "calmly, and appropriately," has been firmly replaced by a sexual world inhabited by "terrible sexual problems," "obscenity," and "complications." Through Romain's story and Felek's explanation, the narrator sees the world of pleasure and desire inextricably united with the world of danger and disease.

This scene offers some insight into the character of Felek as well. When he first hears of Romain's situation, Felek is disgusted, and later becomes embarrassed when the teacher takes the story lightheartedly. After his short discussion with the teacher, he is suddenly able to talk about everything having to do with sexuality and perversion. Though the narrator describes Felek as speaking with "a passionate contempt," it seems to him that Felek "had to and even wanted to talk about it at length and in detail," and that Felek seemed to be speaking from "knowledge or maybe experience." The contrast between Felek's attitude before and after the teacher speaks with him is strange. Within a short space the perversions that Romain's predicament has brought up have gone from embarrassing to a topic that can be unashamedly discussed. Felek is attempting to live up to his teacher's expectations of maturity, though feeling disgust and contempt for the topic.

Soon after this episode, Felek grows distant from his brother. The narrator begins a closer friendship with Ilko, a sixteen-year-old Ukrainian farmhand who works on the manor grounds. In one scene, Ilko takes the narrator to the stables, where he tells him,

> "I'll come here with yer little lordship in spring," said Ilko, "with a lantern, and then there'll be a clamor!"
> "What? What? Ilko, tell me, what will be here in spring?" I asked, excited by the secretive tone of his voice, but Ilko did not want to say.
> "Yer little lordship will see, it's not long to spring!"
> I guessed what he was about, but I wanted Ilko to tell me about it, [. . .] at length, not sparing a single detail. (217)

The narrator, having learned about the wider world of sex earlier from his brother, is now able to guess that Ilko is hinting at catching others having sex in the barn, an idea that excites and arouses him. Though he was confused and repulsed by the earlier conversation, it was this event that made him open to the sexual realm. Not only does he want to hear more about what will take place in the spring, he wants to hear it in "detail" and "at length." The narrator then describes his reaction to this arousal:

> And suddenly I grabbed him around the waist. He wore nothing on his slender fine body except a shirt and a simple tunic. I pressed my hands firmly against his pelvis. He laughed quietly.
> "Let me go, yer lordship," he said languidly. "Let's go downstairs."
> But I didn't let him go, and squeezing him I grasped his leather belt, and grabbed onto it.
> "Yer lordship, carefully," Ilko said unhurriedly. "You'll break my belt. And it's a very beautiful belt." (217)

Having been inducted into the sexual world, the narrator suddenly feels confident enough to act on his desires and instigate a sexual encounter. It is obvious that the narrator is not entirely certain of his own actions, and yet he attempts to take a dominant position, grabbing Ilko by the waist from behind. Ilko seems both willing and experienced in this situation. He laughs, and his replies to the narrator's advances are described as "languid," and "unhurried," adding to the erotic air of the moment.

Within this scene there appears an important class dynamic. As a peasant, Ilko is automatically in a position of subservience to the narrator, who, even though younger by four years, is a member of the Polish gentry, and therefore enjoys a certain amount of power over him. This power relation is further highlighted by the description of Ilko's clothing. He is dressed only in a shirt and tunic, brought together by a belt, owning little else by way of clothing as a peasant in Polish Ukraine. The simplicity of the outfit and its similarity to a dress associates Ilko with a woman. The moment seems to be heading toward a sexual encounter of some kind until the narrator's attention is drawn to Ilko's belt. The narrator asks to see it, describing it as the most beautiful belt he had ever seen. After admiring it he demands Ilko give it to him, to which Ilko replies: "Oho! [. . .] As if the young lord had so few beautiful things" (218). The narrator demands the belt a second time. This upsets Ilko and ruins the erotic moment, ending with the narrator failing in his first attempt at seduction. The narrator's demand for Ilko's belt is first of all an attempt to undress him. However, as he is untrained in seduction, his attempt turns into an overly demanding power play. He forgets that at this moment the more experienced Ilko has more power over him, despite his position as a member of a national minority and potential sexual recipient.

The belt becomes a leitmotif in the course of the novel, tying the erotic to the thanatic as well as becoming a symbol of heterosexist and national power. Already within this scene the narrator has attached an erotic significance to the belt in the narrator's desire for it and his attempt to undress Ilko. Later this erotic attachment is strengthened when the narrator finds Ilko hiding under the teacher's bed. He then takes the belt, which had been lying on the floor. This means that Ilko has finally been undressed, and the narrator gives out a cry of victory, having won both the belt and Ilko's nakedness, finally proving that he is indeed Ilko's better. The belt is ultimately tied to the thanatic in the very last scene of the story when Felek, having discovered the truth of the teacher's sexuality, hangs himself with it.

After the narrator's attempted seduction of Ilko, the relationship between Felek and the teacher sours. The narrator is able to convince Felek to go with him and Ilko to spy on the farmhands and maids having sex in the barns. After several nights of this the teacher notices their tiredness from not getting enough sleep, and eventually catches them one night on their way back from the barns. He asks them from where they are coming, and the narrator boldly admits to watching the farmhands' and maids' sexual activities in the hay. The teacher tells Ilko to leave, but leads the boys home where he interrogates them about their activities. The narrator describes Felek as being "defiant" in his answers, noting a triumphant tone in his voice. Then "the teacher rose: 'Felek, Felek!' he cried. 'How could you so crudely. . .' And suddenly he jumped through the empty dining room, quickly through the hall, waving his hands about his ears" (230). The teacher, in hysterics, runs to his residence, where he begins to cry louder and louder. The narrator and Felek follow after him, and listen at the window. Tellingly, the teacher is only upset by the boys' actions because Felek had taken part in them. As a base and simple peasant Ilko is expected to act "crudely," and therefore does not need to be lectured. However, the teacher's "dramatic" reaction seems to be more than just a guardian's disappointment and approaches the response of a deceived lover. Indeed, Felek's defiant, triumphant manner in relating the details suggests a cruel maliciousness meant solely to hurt the teacher.

Soon after the teacher goes to his rooms, Julcia Wallishauser, an older single woman who had been trying to court the teacher, comes in an effort to comfort him, but he repeatedly tells her to leave him alone. Finally, after her further attempts to comfort him the teacher loses control. "'Leave me in peace!' he yelled, angrily. 'Once and for all give me peace. And I am not "Kazik" to you. I've had enough of this sweetness. Get out!' he suddenly screamed, 'Get out, once and for all get out of my room. Even here you won't give me any peace!'" (232). The hysterical reaction the teacher has to Julcia's attempt to calm him makes quite clear his disinterest in female companionship. Throughout the novel, a number of single women had demonstrated an interest in the teacher, but he had only shown a minor friendliness towards Julcia Wallishauser. With his outburst, it is now obvious that he has no interest not only in Julcia but in any woman. It becomes clear that the kindness he showed her earlier in the novel was only a way to keep the rest of the women from acting on their affection for him. Eventually, the teacher's rejection of Julcia leads to his downfall. His declaration that he has "had enough of this sweetness" is perhaps the most revealing line of this scene. He has no desire for the "sweetness" of women, preferring instead the "coarseness" of men.

After the teacher's outburst, Julcia leaves, and the narrator describes the following scene: "I saw him [Felek] through the open door, kneeling beside the teacher's bed, crying quietly and bitterly along with Mr. Kazimierz" (232). The image this scene creates is rather ambiguous. At first glance it may seem to be the scene of a penitent student, or prodigal son begging forgiveness of his mentor. Taking into account the frivolity and hilarity of Felek's transgression, this reaction by them both seems to be exceedingly hyperbolic. It could also be read as two quarrelling lovers reconciling. This conclusion is supported by the contrast between the teacher's reaction here and his reaction to Romain's earlier description of having caught an STD. In the earlier passage, the teacher finds Romain's situation quite funny, and seems to convince Felek of its hilarity. What has changed between the two scenes is that his beloved, Felek, was involved in the crudity. However, I am unwilling to interpret the relationship between Felek and the teacher as anything physical, taking into account evidence from later in the story. I would suggest that it remains a master/student relationship, though obviously it does become quite emotionally deep. What is more, in carrying on a purely "intellectual" relationship with Felek but a physical one with Ilko, the teacher reinforces the class distinctions at play in the manor.

A revealing passage appears immediately following this scene between the teacher and Felek. The narrator describes how "once again I lost contact with my loony brother, between him and 'Kazimierz' there began an idyll that irritated me. I noticed that Felek was sucking up to the teacher, and I was very sorry for him" (233). It is clear that Felek is now on a first name basis with the teacher. The narrator's description of Felek's "sucking up" to the teacher makes plain his disdain for their relationship. The Polish "*podlizać się*" is quite a loaded term. It is translated as "brown-nosing," "sucking up to," or "kissing up to." However, a literal translation would be "to lick from below," which brings to mind more of the idea of "ass kissing." Iwaszkiewicz's word choice illustrates the intimacy between Felek and the teacher. This is reinforced also by the use of "idyll," which references once again the intellectual ancient Greek teacher/student relationship.

This idyll is destroyed soon after this scene as Julcia involves the narrator in a plan to out the teacher. She takes him to the teacher's residence where they look in on him and see him and Ilko at the table having a lesson. When the teacher closes the windows and shades and puts out the lights, Julcia leaves but tells the narrator to stay and wait. Wasylko, another farmhand, soon appears and knocks on the door. After some time the teacher answers, "his voice coming from the bed" (238). Wasylko tells him that Julcia had sent him, to which the teacher replies, "to hell with Ms. Julcia" (238). Once Wasylko tells him it has to do with Felek, the teacher agrees to come out, locking the door behind him. Wasylko returns to the narrator, who had been hiding, and they enter the teacher's cottage through the window. "The first thing the light of the lantern fell upon was Ilko's red belt, like a cobra lying on the floor" (238–239). The redness and snake-like character of the belt reinforces its erotic and thanatic qualities. It brings to mind both the apple of the Tree of Knowledge as well as the serpent that convinces Adam and Eve to eat it. The narrator picks up the belt and yells victoriously, "she lo-ost her skir-irt! She lo-ost her skir-irt!" (239). Once again, Ilko is associated with a woman. Not only does the narrator use the word "skirt" but he puts the verb "to lose" in the feminine past (zgubiła). Eventually, they find Ilko beneath the bed crying. That the belt was found on the floor means that Ilko had undressed and was in bed with the teacher. During the earlier scene in the barn, Ilko had occupied a position of sexual power over the narrator, though a weaker position in terms of class and nationality. Now that the narrator is in possession of the belt, he holds both sexual and class power over Ilko, who is now in a much weaker position. The belt comes to symbolize nationalist, heteronormative ideology.

Several days later, after a long absence, the father returns to the manor. After lunch the narrator describes watching Ilko walking through the garden

> only in a camisole. [. . .] Julcia and I looked at one another, and then at Mr. Kazimierz. With a clear, cold look he followed Ilko's steps as he slowly walked across the lawn, swaying his free right hand. [. . .] As if waking up, Mr. Kazimierz suddenly looked at me and saw my obstinate gaze and derisive smile. He turned himself towards Julcia, but her small eyes, similar in that moment to the eyes of a snake, were even more horrible. He quickly shifted his own to his plate. (240–241)

The narrator and Julcia have caught the teacher "checking out" Ilko, who is again ascribed feminine qualities, being described as having "light, northern hair" that "flows out like gold, carrying a watering can "swaying his free hand." The description creates an image more similar to that of a country maiden, walking through her garden rather than one of a virile farmhand. It is quite similar to the description of Zosia when she is first seen in "Pan Tadeusz."[11] The narrator then describes Ilko "slowly walking through the scene," as if on the stage of a play, referencing the idyll described earlier throughout the novella.

Having thus caught the teacher, Julcia asks to speak with the father after lunch. This is the first time we discover the father's first name, "Oktawian" or "Octavian." This invokes the image of Gaius Octavius, the emperor of Rome, who was infamous for upholding strict morality in others, even exiling his own granddaughter for adultery. They go into the father's office, where Julcia tells him about the teacher. Wasylko is then ordered in, and then the teacher who walked "as though to the guillotine" (243). Finally, the father announces that the teacher will be leaving immediately, and will not be allowed to say his goodbyes (243). That punishment is so quickly meted out by the father as a result of his panic in perceiving the teacher as a threat to his sons. As a member of the gentry, he believes it to be his duty to make sure his sons help in maintaining the nation. This is made clear earlier in the story, when it is revealed that the oldest son is away fighting in the Polish-Soviet War of 1920. In order to support the nation, the boys must remain "intact," impenetrable, and go on to partake in the marriage myth.

Iwaszkiewicz describes a Poland in which the nationalist and heteronormative regimes are so restrictive that even a person who works to instill patriotism in his students cannot be forgiven for his transgressive sexuality. Earlier in the story the narrator says of the teacher that he "spoke very beautifully about Poland, but did not go to war for her, staying in our Ukrainian manor, like with the Lord God behind the oven. (In regard to this I was unfair: he was killed in 1920)" (233). Despite his obvious love for Poland, even eventually fighting and dying for the nation, he cannot be tolerated within the national structure. The father's panic is in stark contrast to his attitude toward the teacher from earlier in the story as he watched him lead Felek and a group of men in putting out a fire. The father remarks, "'Look at Felek,' he said. 'How he works. [. . .] I never thought he had it in him.'" The mother replies, "He was never like that. Mr. Kazimierz has brought out his true character" (223–224). They both express pride in their son's bravery and acknowledge that it is because of the teacher's influence on Felek that he has become a man. The mother even tells the teacher, in stereotypically dramatic fashion, "Now I know to whom I could entrust my boys if I were to die" (224). However, in the end, because of his "polluted" body, the teacher is not allowed to partake in the nation. He has been found to be penetrable, and therefore untrustworthy as a man. Despite having proven his "masculinity" and his patriotism, the teacher remains nothing more than a "*Puto*" in the eyes of the regimes of heteronormativity.[12]

Later, when the two brothers are in their room, Felek finally asks why the teacher has been let go. The narrator says, "his questions irritated me. I would answer. How could Felek be so stupid as not to know what was going on around him?" (245). The younger brother has become worldlier than the older. Wasylko then comes in to ask for Ilko's belt, and we learn that Ilko has also been let go. Felek gives Wasylko ten rubles in gold for the belt, and, "began closely looking at the crimson strap as if his history were written in runes on the leather" (245). Felek's encounter with the belt is fateful. The "runes" etched into it describe the nationalist imperative for punishing queer desire. When he takes possession of it, it is the culmination of the clash between *Eros* and *Thanatos*. Around Ilko's waist it had been the locus of desire by both the narrator and the teacher. When the narrator discovers it on the floor, it reveals that the teacher's desires have been fulfilled. This, however, cannot be tolerated, and now the belt will function as the thanatic instrument to punish this transgression of the homosocial pact. The narrator then tells Felek the meaning of the belt rather derisively. "Guessing what it meant for Felek, I purposely, maliciously paused at certain details, even adding a thing or two" (246).

The roles of the two brothers change in this passage. Whereas Felek was the more knowledgeable in the earlier scene involving Romain, the narrator is now more in control of the language of sex, desire, and power. It seems that suddenly the narrator has aged in experience more than his older brother, as he now uses "cynical," "crude" language to describe the details, which are tellingly once again left unwritten. He very consciously speaks in such a way, even making up some details, in order to hurt Felek, being annoyed by his brother's naiveté.

Felek is devastated by the teacher's dismissal. When he finally discovers why the teacher has been fired, he hangs himself with the belt Ilko had lost while hiding under the teacher's bed. Like his father, Felek also experiences homosexual panic. Before his discovery of the teacher's sexuality theirs had been a relationship of student and teacher. After his discovery this relationship is somehow sullied and must now be questioned. In the final scene between him and the teacher, Felek is forced to confront the possibility of his own homosexuality, which then produces his panic:

> "Felek, Felek, you must understand, you must understand me and yourself."
> "Understand? Understand what?" the boy yelled angrily. "Understand that everything, everything . . . such happiness. . . that our entire friendship was just. . . was just. . ."
> "Be quiet, quiet," Kazimierz cried begging, suddenly changing his tone and abruptly stifled Felek's words with his lips.
> Felek shuddered and fell quiet. Mr. Kazimierz slowly kissed the tears that were flowing down his cheeks, kissing his eyes, eyebrows, and forehead. (247)

Iwaszkiewicz plays with many levels of ambiguity in this passage, which again speaks to the ineffability of queer love. The phrase "abruptly stifled Felek's words with his lips" seems overly descriptive. It can only mean that the teacher is kissing Felek full on the mouth, and yet it remains impossible to describe unambiguously the act of two men kissing. It must remain buried beneath metaphor. The word "kiss" does appear later, though now the teacher is simply kissing Felek's cheeks, eyes, eyebrows, and forehead. Furthermore, the teacher's statement "you must understand me and yourself" adds to the ambiguity. It may simply be the teacher telling Felek that he must understand the situation, and that he can no longer stay at the manor. In my opinion, what the teacher is suggesting is that Felek must understand both the teacher's and his own sexuality and accept it. Though this is the first time their relationship has taken on any kind of physical character, they have undoubtedly formed a strong emotional bond. Despite never having engaged in sex, there is love, and quite possibly desire felt between them. It is this love that cannot be tolerated by the regime of the Father. When Felek states, "understand that [. . .] such happiness . . . that our entire friendship was just . . . was just . . ." his stuttering illustrates the impossibility of uttering the truth of such desires. It must remain unspoken, and ambiguous. At the end of the scene, Felek jumps out the window and runs away, later hanging himself with Ilko's belt. Felek kills himself due to the panic he feels from the mere possibility of his queer desires, and therefore having unforgivably transgressed the boundaries of the homosocial into the realm of the homosexual.

TRANSATLANTYK

Witold Gombrowicz's *TransAtlantyk*, unlike *The Teacher*, needs no introduction. There are pages of bibliographies dedicated to it. Despite the amount of scholarship, an intersectional analysis along the axis of national and gender identity transgression has the potential to reveal something new about the novella. In contrast to *The Teacher*, which is set in the Polish homeland, *TransAtlantyk* takes place outside the nation, among the Polish diaspora of Buenos Aires. The novel begins on the eve of the Second World War, and so the stability of the nation is immediately under threat. This literal threat will later be accompanied by the symbolic threat of homoerotic desire. Gombrowicz-the-character is disembarking from the ship *Chrobry* after a voyage from Poland, during which time he describes himself as feeling like "a man in-between" (1994, 3).[13] Introduced at the very beginning, this "in-between-ness" will become an important theme throughout the novel. As Ewa Płonowska-Ziarek points out in *Gombrowicz's Grimaces* (1998a),[14] this notion of existing "in-between" is important in much of Gombrowicz's work and life. As he says in *Testament: Entretiens de Dominique de Roux avec Gombrowicz* (1977), "these 'betweens' [. . .] multiplied until they almost constituted my country of residence, my true home" (qtd. in Płonowska-Ziarek 1998a, 28). This designation of the "in-between" as a kind of "nation" acts as a critique of the concept of the stable, monolithic nation-state. Gomrowicz's nation, as the setting of the story, is a liminal space, open to instabilities.

After hearing about Germany's invasion of Poland, the Polish delegation decides to return to Europe, hoping to make it at least to England in order to help in the war effort. Gombrowicz, however, refuses to go back, saying, "'Here I will stay!' Thus I speak mumbling (as the whole truth I could not say)" (5). He says goodbye to his friend Czesław, thinking "though as if some Secret were between us" (6). Once again, just as in *The Teacher*, a theme of silence and the inexpressible appears; however, instead of an inability to express queer desire, Gombrowicz is unable to express his desire for freedom from the nation. He gives voice to this later as, watching the ship sail away, he says to himself,

> Sail, sail, you Compatriots, to your People! Sail to that holy Nation of yours haply Cursed! Sail to that St. Monster Dark, dying for ages yet unable to die! Sail to your St. Freak, cursed by all Nature, ever being born and still Unborn! Sail, sail, so he will not suffer you to Live or Die but keep you for ever between Being and Non-being. (7)

From the very beginning of the novel the entire category of "Poland" is put into doubt. Gombrowicz repudiates the Romantic messianism that had defined "Polish-ness" since the eighteenth century, and refuses the nationalist demand for self-sacrifice for the nation. As Płonowska-Ziarek states, "Unlike the opening invocation [. . .] of *Pan Tadeusz* in which the lost country is nostalgically extolled as the source of life, Gombrowicz's novel opens with a mockingly blasphemous curse of the nation and with the betrayal of the patriotic ethos" (1998b, 225). His description of Poland as "St. Monster Dark," "St. Freak," and as "dying for ages yet unable to die" is the anti-messianic answer to the designation of Poland as "Christ of Nations," which, as Knut Grimstad explains, was "the haunted idea of Messianism, which, in its extreme form, presented Poland as the collective Christ, crucified to redeem the nations, one day to be resurrected by a new embodiment of the Holy Spirit" (Grimstad and Phillips 2005, 9).[15] This theme would become a powerful, central metaphor for the Polish Romantics in both their work and their lives, invoking it several times in (failed) attempts to rally revolution against the colonizing Russians.

The departing Poles tell Gombrowicz that he should announce himself to the Polish Legation so that he will not be taken for a deserter. He finds an old friend, a Pan Cieciszowski to ask his advice, who tells him, "I'm not so mad as to have any views These Days or not to have them" (8). His advice becomes a farcical spiral of positive statement and negation:

> Get ye anon to the Legation or do not get ye there and Report your presence there or do not Report. [. . .] Do whatever you opine [. . .] or do not opine [. . .] but do not go to them 'cause if they stick to you they will not come unstuck! Take my Counsel, you had better to keep with Foreigners. [. . .] God forbid that you shun the Legation or Compatriots living here. (8)

Cieciszwoski's tirade becomes, as George Gasyna puts it, "a miniature treatise on émigré ambivalence" (2011, 153). Having already lived in Buenos Ares, for a time, Cieciszowski has come to understand the liminality of the immigrant experience, being outside the homeland, and yet being "stuck" within the expatriate community. He is also well aware that whether or not Gombrowicz announces his presence to the Legation, "they will Bite, [him] they will bite to bits!" (8). Despite being outside the nation proper he remains subject to their national imaginary. Gaytri Gopinath notes that "while the diaspora within nationalist discourse is often positioned as the abjected and disavowed Other to the nation, the nation also simultaneously recruits the diaspora into its absolutist logic" (2005, 7). The diaspora is often "complicit" in the formation and maintenance of nationalism, at times engaging in these regimes more resolutely than the nation itself.

Gombrowicz finally decides to go to the Legation, and visits "His Excellency the Envoy." After an attempt to ask for employment they begin discussing the war, saying, "'The War,' say I. He says: 'The war.' Say I: 'The war.' He to this: 'The War.' So I to him: 'The War, the war'" (13). This leads the envoy to exclaim,

> We will vanquish the enemy! [. . .] We will, by my troth. I say this to you, and I say this so you cannot say that I was saying that we would not Vanquish, since I say to you that we will Vanquish, will Win, for we will reduce to dust with our mighty, gracious hand—smash, crush to dust, powder, with Sabres, Lances anatomize, annihilate, demolish! [. . .] And don't you dare bark thus: that I didn't Pace before you, that I didn't Say, as you see that I do Pace and Say! (13)

These exaggerated exclamations appear throughout the novel in order to parody the "empty gestures" Gombrowicz continually comes across among the Polish émigré community. He repeats "Empty! Empty!" over and again as a kind of lament at being accosted with these pathetic expressions of patriotism. The envoy does not necessarily believe that Poland will be victorious; he merely makes theses proclamations so that Gombrowicz "cannot say that [he] was saying that we would not Vanquish" (13). Such "empty" gestures critique the absurdity of nationalist and normative discourses that rely on arbitrary expressions of patriotism to maintain nationalist regimes of control.

The two previous passages also demonstrate that being part of an émigré community does not lessen the effect of the threat to the male body/nation, and the necessity of the members of that community to remain adherent to the national norms. George Gasyna notes that patriotic agencies such as the Legation "provide a moral compass for émigré comportment and enforce its sense of group identity by dictum [. . .] in an effort to reinforce a communal identity but also and principally as an exercise in power politics that figuratively extends the zone of the fatherland beyond its legislated [. . .] borders" (154). Immigrant communities, despite being outside the nation proper, are often even more invested in maintaining nationalist regimes than citizens living within the nation itself. The fantasy of the whole, stable nation within the diasporic imagination is necessary for the endurance of a national identity outside the geographic bounds of the nation. Cieciszowski's inability to express simple, straightforward opinion, and the envoy's need to voice hyperbolic and highly scripted platitudes of patriotism, both point to the diaspora's need for maintaining and monitoring the émigré community's devotion to the fatherland.

Soon after his meeting with the envoy, Gombrowicz is forced to attend a reception, where he is paraded as a "national genius" in front of Argentineans, and where he has a duel of words with a character who is a thinly veiled representation of Jorge Luis Borges. This "duel of words" will later be mirrored by an actual duel. It too will descend into farce, satirizing the Polish nationalist desire for "defending manhood." After failing in his duel with "Borges," Gombrowicz begins "pacing" in defiance of both Polish émigré culture and the Argentinean literati. During his pacing the character Gonzalo appears at his side. He discovers that Gonzalo is a "puto," "Mestizo, Portuguese, of a Persian-Turkish mother in Libya born" (37). Similarly to Gombrowicz, Gonzalo is also "in-between" in both his sexuality and ethnicity. The character of Gonzalo becomes the very embodiment of the "trans" in the novel's title. His ethnic "identity" is nearly an impossibility, magically coalescing without regard even to geographical distances. He also defiantly transgresses normative sexuality, openly pursuing young men. Later in the novel, his estate, which I discuss later, becomes an analogue of his "transness," embodied in his pets, which are the fantastical offspring of dogs and rats, as well as in the decoration of his house, which is made up of clashing, incoherent styles.

After pacing with him, Gonzalo attempts to befriend Gombrowicz, telling him about his desire for younger men. He sees one such boy he has had his eye on for a while speaking with an older man in a park. They follow them to a dance hall and Gombrowicz realizes the two men are Poles. Gonzalo pleads with Gombrowicz to approach them. He finally acquiesces, and introduces himself. "Herewith the Old Gentleman to me: that to the army he is dispatching his Only Son, the which, if unable to reach our Country, would enlist in England or in France, so that from this side he could wrack the enemy" (49). Tomasz, the Old Gentleman, is a representative of the Poland Gombrowicz had attacked earlier in the novel. He is completely invested in the Romantic belief in self-sacrifice for the nation, and is willing to send his "Only Son" off to war to fight and probably die for Poland.

While Gombrowicz sits with Tomasz and Ignacy, Gonzalo begins "drinking to" Ignacy. When Tomasz asks to whom he is drinking, Gombrowicz replies, "To Ignasio, to Ignasio. [. . .] Hie thee hence, hie thee hence with your Son else you'll expose yourself to people's raillery!" (49). However, Tomasz replies, "I with Ignacy [. . .] will not flee as my Ignacy is not a maiden!" (49). Because of the queer threat, Tomasz must assert Ignacy's manhood, and that such a threat cannot undermine him. Instead of running Tomasz stands against Gonzalo's "drinking," eventually leading the distraught Gonzalo to throw his glass at the wall behind Tomasz, cutting his head. Soon after, Tomasz tells Gombrowicz, "I must challenge him. I will duel with him so that this matter in a manly manner betwixt Men is settled; to be sure, I will make a Man of him that it cannot be said that a Puto is after my son! Ergo, if he does not stand up to me, I will shoot him as a Dog, and you tell him so, so that he knows. He must stand up to me!" (54). The language Tomasz uses to rationalize his challenge to Gonzalo is repeated later by another minister of the legation when he is told of the impending duel: "'tis important, gentlemen, that that Manliness of ours is not hidden under a bushel, [. . .] so, whilst over there, in our Country, Heroism is extraordinary today, let people over here see how a Pole can stand up!" (64). In both passages the notion of "Manliness" (with a capital M) takes central importance. The Polish émigré community is highly invested in this expression and defense of manhood. Gombrowicz realizes that they have "contrived a Hero," that this pretense of manliness and patriotism is simply another "empty" pose that serves no productive purpose. The pose is no more than a ridiculous gesture meant to reify received notions of messianic nationalism. For Tomasz a show of his manliness is necessary in order to repel the queer threat to his son, while the minister voices his support of this show of manliness as he believes it will somehow support the nationalist mission in the homeland.

Tomasz's reaction to Gonzalo's advances illustrates Sedgwick's theory of homosexual panic. Being a patriot, the father must eliminate this threat to his son's impenetrable unity, especially as he wishes to send him back to Europe to fight the invading Germans and Soviets. It is made clear that he would rather his son die in Poland's defense than be "corrupted," or polluted by a homosexual. As Płonowska-Ziarek points out, "Ignacy's father attempts to restore the heterosexual identity of his son and to save national honor by reinscribing male eroticism within ritualized, and already obsolete structures of aggressive rivalry," and within these rituals Gonzalo is not allowed "the luxury of being both a gay man and staying alive" (1998b, 232). The minister's mirroring of this sentiment creates a link between the male body and the nation, illustrating the heteronormative, nationalist desire for both to remain stable and closed systems. Just as in *The Teacher* the expression of queer desire in Gombrowicz's novel leads to a thanatic response; however, this time instead of a person taking their own life, in *TransAtlantyk* homosexual panic leads to the desire for murder.

Gombrowicz is chosen to officiate the duel and so must inform Gonzalo of the challenge. Gonzalo pleads with Gombrowicz for help, suggesting that "instead of siding with the old Father, with the Young Ones [he'd] best join, to the Young Ones some freedom give, and the Young One from Lord Father's Tyranny protect!" (56). For Gonzalo the regime of "Lord Father" is a continuation of the Romantic, messianic cult of death that Gombrowicz rails against at the beginning of the novel. The exchange that follows is one of the most important of the entire novel:

> "[D]o you not acknowledge Progress? Are we to step in place? And how can there be aught New if just to the Old you give credence? Eternally then is Lord Father to hold a young son under his paternal lash? [. . .] Give some slack to the Young One, let him out free rein, let him frisk!"
> [...]
> Speak I: "You madman! For progress I am too, but you call Deviation progress."
> Replied he to this: "But if to deviate a bit, well?" (56)

In contrast to his earlier position, Gombrowicz's narrator is here defending nationalist, heteronormative regimes against Gonzalo's call for youth, deviation, and progress. Of course, if he were truly the patriotic Pole he claims to be, he would have left Argentina with the rest of the Poles at the very beginning of the novel. Gonzalo equates deviation with progress, deviation being a transgression of the bounds between the homosocial and the homosexual. Gonzalo's suggestion then is that deviance, turning away from norms, may well be the most productive force for Poland. Gombrowicz continues to refuse Gonzalo saying, "Say I: 'I would not be a Pole if I were to set a Son against a Father [. . .] and, moreover for Deviation sake.' Exclaimed he: 'But wherefore need you be a Pole?'" (56–57). This is a quite serious question. Why must one remain a Pole, or any nationality? It contests the assumption that the nation is "the most natural and organic subdivision of humanity" (Leerssen 2006, 14).[16] It suggests instead the slippage inherent in "national" identities, and that one's identity need not be based at all on what country in which one happens to be born. Gonzalo goes on to make his case for embracing this rebellious deviance:

> Has the lot of the Poles up to now been so delightful? Has not your Polishness become loathsome to you? Have you not had your fill of Sorrow? Your fill of Soreness, Sadness? [. . .] Would you not become something Else, something New? Would you have all these Boys of yours but just repeat everything forever after Fathers? Oh, release Boys from the paternal cage. Let them veer off the path, let them peer into the Unknown! Thus far the old Father that colt of his has ridden bare and guided according to his own design . . . and now let the colt take the bit between the teeth so that he carries his Father where he will! And then the Father's eyes will nigh whiten for his own Son doth carry him, carry him away! Gee-up, go! Give free rein to those Boys of yours, let them Gallop, let them Run, let them Bolt and be Carried away! (57)

Gonzalo's call for rebelling against "Fathers," with capital "F," is a call for an end to the masochistic cycle of death that nationalism and heteronormativity had created. For Gonzalo the Polish ethic has become one of debasement, and self-denial. He challenges Gombrowicz to become "something new," to attempt to exit this destructive pattern. His suggestion is to end the reign of the fathers, and to allow the sons to "run free," to allow joy back into the world. In light of the situation of Poland of the time, where once again "they are flaying your skins," Gonzalo's question of "Wherefore need you be a Pole?" becomes quite poignant.

Gonzalo punctuates his argument with the following statement: "To the Devil with Pater and Patria! The Son, the son's the thing, oh, indeed! But wherefore need you Patria? Is not Filistria better? You exchange Patria for Filistria and then you'll see!" (57). These two passages become the very thesis of *TransAtlantyk*. "The Son's the thing" will become another echo, similar to that of "Empty! Empty!" to which Gombrowicz continually returns. This is also the first moment the term "Patria" is used, or in the original Polish "Ojczyzna," literally "Fatherland." "Ojczyzna" is always already pregnant with meaning in Polish literature. Its mention automatically references the first line of "Pan Tadeusz": "O! Lithuania, O! my fatherland!" Gonzalo then creates the word "Filistria," or "Synczyzna," literally "the Sonland" in opposition to "Fatherland." Gonzalo becomes a disruptive character who attempts to subvert notions of stability and uniformity championed by the Father. For him the Father, or "ojczyzna" is equivalent to tradition, death, and enslavement, while the Son, or "synczyzna" is equivalent to progress, life, and individual freedom. His arguments begin to convince the narrator, who will struggle for the rest of the novel between helping maintain the strict heteronormative system of the "ojczyzna," or instead allowing the "synczyzna" to explore new pleasures and identities. Gombrowicz's ideas on the productive energies of adolescence as opposed to the static character of maturity were a major concern throughout much of his work, especially in his first important novel, *Ferdydurke* (2000).

For the moment Gombrowicz decides to work against the ojczyzna, realizing that it is no more than a repetition of past Romantic nationalist systems that lead only to death. During the duel he does not load either pistol with shot, a plan he had discussed with other Polish émigrés who had agreed to it as it would prove complicated if Tomasz were arrested for murder. The father demands they repeat the duel until one of them is dead. The scene quickly turns into absurdity as the two men repeatedly fire unloaded weapons at one another. Through this farcical scene Gombrowicz subverts the regimes of heteronormativity, revealing the ridiculousness of their homophobic paranoia. The duel becomes a satire lampooning Polish patriarchy and nationalism. It is the epitome of the "empty" gesture Gombrowicz continually laments throughout the novel. Since everyone except the father understands the emptiness and meaninglessness of the scene, Gombrowicz has made the only seriously invested representative of the Patria the butt of a joke (82–85).

The repeated shooting of empty pistols by Gonzalo and Tomasz only finally ends when Ignacy is nearly mauled by a pack of dogs, and is then saved by Gonzalo who "at those Dogs hurled himself, and did with bare hands, yet with a cry Terrible, heaven-piercing [. . .] tearing them away from that Ignasiek of his, him with his own body, with his own body shielding!" (77). At first Tomasz is grateful to Gonzalo for saving his son, but later he will voice concerns about his "terrible cry," which Tomasz believes to have been too "woman-like." All having been forgiven for the time being, Gonzalo invites Tomasz, Ignacy, and Gombrowicz for lunch to his estate, where the incoherent excess astounds them. Gonzalo's manor is filled with expensive works of art of every kind, but placed in no discernible order, stacked one on top of another. When asked about "these Treasures," he replies: "Aye, treasures [. . .] and this is why, sparing no cost, all I bought and here did gather, did pile that they might Cheapen for me a bit. Ergo, these Masterpieces, Paintings, Statues together here enclosed, one the other Cheapening by its excess" (80–81). Instead of carefully displaying the works of art he has collected, Gonzalo decides to simply pile them one on top of another in hopes of cheapening their value. It is an act utterly antithetical to the more common goal of buying art so that it will appreciate in value. Gonzalo is attempting to delineate an oppositional space that stands in contrast to normative modes of structure and form. Form and borders are impossible in the chaos of his estancia. This chaos is punctuated further by the "Dogs" that inhabit his manor. Gombrowicz describes, "a little dog across the hall scampers, a Bolognese, although it seems that with a Poodle crossed since a poodle's tail it had and the hair of a Fox-terrier. [. . .] [T]wo Dogs, one of which an imp, Pekinese, but with brush-tail, and the other Shepherd (but as if with a rat's tail and Bulldog's muzzle)" (81). Later these "breeds" become even more fantastical. Tomasz notices one:

> belike a Setter, but a meager lop-ear 'tis for as if a Hamster's ears it has. Replied Gonzalo that a Wolfhound Bitch he had, the which in the Cellar with a Hamster must have coupled, and although afterwards mated with a Setter, pups with a Hamster's Ears had whelped. [. . .] "A bitch I had, St. Bernard with a pointer, a Spitz laced, but apparently with Cat Tom somewhere in the cellars it must have coupled." (82)

Gonzalo's estate is a liminal space in which all borders become fluid and meaningless. By stacking his valuable artworks in such a random, contrasting manner he hopes to cheapen them, and at the same time attempts to destroy the structures of genre and style connected with art. The dogs he has "bred" are the impossible results of couplings not just between dissimilar breeds, but even between different species. Gombrowicz later describes it as a place of "incessant blending" (97), where he drinks "beer; but not beer as, although Beer, perchance with wine laced; and Cheese not Cheese, aye Cheese, but as if not Cheese. Next those pâtés, perchance Layer Pastries, and as if Pretzel or Marzipan; not Marzipan though, but perchance Pistachio although made of liver" (83). In Gonzalo's estate received assumptions of reality play no role in the ontological character of things. It is a place where a dog breed can be the combination of a hamster and cat, and where beer is beer, but at the same time it is not-beer.

Gombrowicz becomes disturbed by the fluidity and instability of Gonzalo's *estancia*. He finally confesses to Tomasz, telling him the truth about the duel. Tomasz is dumbfounded, unable to accept that he had fired with no shot in the pistol. He then tells Gombrowicz that he plans on killing his own son. For Tomasz, Ignacy's penetrated body will no longer be of any use to the nation. Indeed, it will become a detriment to it, and therefore killing him becomes the only solution. Gombrowicz realizes that Tomasz and his homosexual panic are "likewise Empty" as the other meaningless gestures of nationalism that have confronted him. He then tells Gonzalo of Tomasz's plan, who in turn plans on convincing Ignacy to kill his father.

The murderous plots of both Tomasz and Gonzalo create a moral conundrum for Gombrowicz. Despite his disdain for regimes of Polish chauvinism, it remains difficult for him to partake in subverting the *ojczyzna* in favor of the *synczyzna*. Seemingly in response to his indecision, three other Poles suddenly abduct Gombrowicz, thrusting a spur into his calf, and he passes out from the pain. When he awakes, he finds himself in a cellar with the three Poles who had abducted him. These three all have terrible spurs on their boots. Gombrowicz notices that any time one of them makes any movement one of the other two jab him with their spur. Another character, the Accomptant comes in, orders that a spur be affixed to Gombrowicz's boot, then explains:

> Now to our Order of the Chevaliers of the Spur you belong. [. . .] Do not attempt an escape or any betrayal as with a Spur they will prod you, and if you notice the faintest wish to Betray, to Escape, in any of your Comrades, into him a Spur you must shove. And if you neglect doing this, into you they will shove it. And if the one who is to give you a Spur neglects doing this, another one is to give him a Spur. Keep an eye on yourself then, and on others keep an eye. (100)

This passage illustrates the kind of power relations that Foucault describes in his work *Discipline and Punish* (1995). Instead of power as a top down system, his analysis portrays power as a circular, self-monitoring system in which everyone plays a part. The scene is a satire aimed at regimes of control. It is first of all a lampoon of the kind of paranoid police states that Hitler and Stalin had installed, where everyone is a spy spying on everyone else. It also speaks to heteronormative regimes that use homophobia in creating and maintaining homosexual panic in its subjects as a means to sustain national structures. The very name of the group, "The Chevaliers of the Spur," references clandestine secret societies which saw it as their mission to maintain the nation. The irony of this regime of control is the number of times the national, specifically male body must be penetrated in order to control it. It actually reflects a complete permeability of the body. Though it is supposed to be a system of control of the body, it ends up repeatedly penetrating that body, opening it up quite literally to pollution. Despite the apparent absurdities in this system it remains highly effective in controlling subjects, illustrated when Gombrowicz realizes that "my Friends were imprisoning me, and the door was not even locked: just arise and depart" (100–101). Though escape may seem like a rather simple proposition, the threat of violence and the very existence of a self-regulating system itself make it nearly impossible.

Eventually Gombrowicz discovers the impetus behind the creation of the Chevaliers of the Spur. The Accomptant had been ashamed by the fact that Tomasz and Gonzalo had fought a duel with no bullets loaded. He sees this as a betrayal of that Polish "Manliness" that they had been so invested in. To correct this, he founds this "Order of Anguish and Suffering" in order to "redeem" the émigré community. He calls for "Potency, Potency, Potency!" (103). Once again Gombrowicz satirizes the masochism inherent in the Romantic notion of Poles and Poland being the Christ of Nations. Since the homeland is suffering from the war, the diasporic community must maintain a strict adherence to nationalist ideals of Manhood and "Polishness." When they fail to live up to these standards their only recourse is to suffer. With the repetition of "Potency" Gombrowicz indicts the chauvinistic "manliness" that leads to empty "masculine" gestures, such as the earlier duel, as the force behind this masochistic impulse. Through this passage he provides a biting analysis of Poles' self-destructive character, returning the reader back to the beginning of the novel when he refused to return to Europe to fight in the war. The desire for suffering and the expression of "overpowering potency" are also, ultimately, the reasons Tomasz wishes to send his son off to war, which would almost inevitably end in his death. He so desires this expression of manhood that he would even rather kill his own son than see him seduced by a homosexual.

Eventually the cell becomes crowded with almost every Polish character that had thus far appeared in the novel. Gombrowicz finally escapes by telling the rest that they need a more dreadful act to achieve the potency they so desire. He convinces them that he will kill Ignacy, since "death to that youth for no cause given will be a more awesome death than any other" (107), which the group heartily agrees to. When he finally returns to the estate, he is about to warn Ignacy of Gonzalo's plans to kill his father and to then seduce him. He stops himself at the last second, realizing that if he ruins Gonzalo's trap, what then? Again all as of old, as it was? Again then he beside Lord Father will be, and still after Lord Father prayers will prate. [. . .] Still on and on, over and over, again the same? [. . .] Give then some free-rein to the boy. May he do Whatever he Would! [. . .] Let him sin! [. . .] may all Break, Burst, Fall apart, Fall apart, and oh, Filistria Becoming, Unknown Filistria! (115)

Gombrowicz has finally accepted that to take the side of the Father and Patria is to help maintain the cycle of death these institutions had been upholding for generations, to support a "leprous tribe in love with death" (Warkocki, 2019). All he had seen out of the Ojczyzna were empty gestures and poses of manliness that had led to nothing but more threats of punishment and death. Whether for good or bad he is willing to allow "deviation" and youth the chance to change the world. He has finally taken seriously the question Gonzalo posed: "Wherefore need you be a Pole?"

The novel ends with nothing truly being resolved, seemingly collapsing in on itself with its absurdities. Gombrowicz sees the compatriots he had left in the cellar riding each other like horses. He then learns that Poland has fallen to Germany. In a move reminiscent of the ending of "Pan Tadeusz," in which the characters dance the Polonaise off into exile, the Poles in Argentina also decide to dance.[17] The last words of the novel are a "Bim! Bam! Boom" of laughter from all the Poles, a final empty gesture in the face of the oblivion they refuse to accept.

CONCLUSION

Sedgwick's theory of homosexual panic illustrates quite well the connection between the formations of national and gender identities. Ultimately, in the examples examined here, homosexual panic is a recursive nationalist panic. The nation is imagined in relation to others, both external and internal. In order for the nation to remain intact and homogenous it must ignore and repress minorities, whether national, ethnic, or sexual. Those who reveal the actual heterogeneity of the nation are kept from participating in it. When the homosocial bonds that make the nation possible are transgressed by queer desires, it threatens the entire notion of the stability of the nation as conceived by nationalist heteronormative regimes. In both *The Teacher* and *TransAtlantyk* we witness the results of the panic created by this threat. In *The Teacher*, Iwaszkiewicz illustrates the violence that is a fundamental result of such paranoia, while in *TransAtlantyk*, Gombrowicz effectively uses the grotesque to subvert both nationalism and compulsory heterosexuality. Just as Iwaszkiewicz's story ties the erotic to the thanatic so too does Gombrowicz's. The desires of Gonzalo for Ignacy are threatened with death at the very start of Gonzalo's attempted seduction, and later lead to conspiracies of murder. However, whereas in *The Teacher* erotic desires lead to tragedy, *TransAtlantyk* ends in an absurd booming laughter.

It is important to note the centrality war plays in the plots of both texts. In *The Teacher* the Polish-Soviet War of 1919 to 1921 is continually lurking in the background, first with the mention that the oldest (unnamed) son is fighting the Soviets, then later when it is revealed that the teacher eventually dies fighting in the same war. In *TransAtlantyk*, the Second World War begins the very action of the novel, immediately splitting the narrator off from his homeland. Both wars, as almost any war, were battles over geographic borders. The Polish-Soviet War was an expansionist project that saw Poland actually temporarily gain territory, something not seen in history since the Union of Lublin in the sixteenth century.

The centrality of the manor house is also important in both texts. In reading Gombrowicz, German Ritz notes that, "Within the landed-estate culture's conception of self, homosexuality may well be a part of male nature, but not a way of life in its own right. The license which allows the experience of desire, does not jeopardize the nobleman's identity. It can become part of the 'gawęda,' that is part of the estate's own lingo, and is therefore integrable" (1996, 262). In the examples from Gombrowicz I would certainly agree with this. For Gombrowicz the manor is a space where regimes of control seemingly break down, seen in both Gonzalo's estancia as well as in the manor house he describes in his first novel *Ferdydurke*. In the earlier work there seems to be the possibility for more acceptance of queer desire as Miętus's attempts at "fraternization" with a farmhand are accepted (2000, 239).[18] This view of the manor house remains true in *TransAtlantyk*, where Gombrowicz takes the symbol further as in the space outside the nation limitations of any kind cease to exist. However, it is obvious that Iwaszkiewicz's view of the manor is not as fluid. Instead of being a space where social restrictions are more flexible, the same constraints against queer desires remain, though perhaps here they are a bit easier to hide. For Iwaszkiewicz the Polish country manor is still Poland, just in miniature.

As is obvious in this analysis, *The Teacher*, as a realist text, is a much less dense work than the more surrealist *TransAtlantyk*. Despite its plainer style, its concerns with nationalist and heteronormative regimes are just as compelling. On the one hand, since Gombrowicz wrote *TransAtlantyk* abroad he was certainly freer to discuss non-normative sexualities more openly than Iwaszkiewicz would have been able to. Despite the story being written and taking place outside the bounds of the nation, it is also clear that Gombrowicz is commenting on the undeniable influence the homeland has on diasporic communities. Ultimately both works become political statements against the systems of homophobia and pathological nationalism that would see fathers, at home and abroad, prefer to sacrifice their sons than see them deviate from their heterosexual and heteronormative duties.

NOTES

1. Błażej Warkocki (2019) also makes use of Sedgwick's theory of homosexual panic to analyze a work by Gombrowicz, the short story "The Events on the Banbury" from the collection *Bacacay*.

2. The "Kresy" was the name given to the multi-ethnic Eastern Borderlands situated between Poland and Russia from 1918, when Poland regained its independence, and 1939, at the start of the Second World War. Kate Brown (2004) discusses the unique geographic, geopolitical, multi-ethnic, and multi-national character of this space.

3. "My specifications of widespread, endemic male homosexual panic as a post-Romantic phenomenon, rather than as coeval with the beginnings, under homophobic pressure, of a distinctive male homosexual culture a century or so earlier, has to do with (what I read as) the centrality of the paranoid Gothic as the literary genre in which homophobia found its most apt and ramified embodiment" (Sedgwick 1990, 186).

4. "The first ritual took place in Puck on February 10, 1920, when general Józef Haller threw a platinum ring into the waters and put another one on his finger, proclaiming he was 'taking possession' of the sea in the name of the Polish Commonwealth. [. . .] This matrimonial gesture was repeated in March 1945 in Kołobrzeg, after the city had been liberated from the Germans" (Sikora 2004, 67).

5. He then goes on to provide a clumsy misreading of the text suggesting the teacher "depraved the oldest of his students" (582). In the following analysis of the novella, I illustrate why it is impossible to arrive at this conclusion.

6. See Tomasik (2008).

7. See the timeline of Iwaszkiewicz's life at the Stawisko Museum's website: http://www.stawisko.pl. "1920–*Pracuje jako nauczyciel domowy u ks. Woronieckich*" (1920–Works as a live-in teacher for the Duke and Duchess Woroniecki).

8. In her analysis of the novella, Ewa Chudoba calls Romain's affliction "*syfilis*" ["syphilis"] (232). However, I find no textual evidence that specifically names the disease. In my opinion it is a further example of Iwaszkiewicz trying to maintain an air of ambiguity and ineffability within the work.

9. "*In* Nauczyciel *ist die Nähe des Erzählers zur erotischen Interaktion zwar grösser, sie wird aber durch die frühpubertäre Unerfahrenheit des Knaben, der sich erzählend an den Skandal des homosexuellen Hauslehrers erinnert, neutralisiert*" (1996, 99–100).

10. See Sedgwick's discussion of "The Beast in the Jungle," and her analysis of John Marcher's "secret," whose "content is homosexual" (201).

11. Adam Mickiewicz, "Pan Tadeusz," lines 81–107.

12. In Gombrowicz's *TransAtlantyk*, "puto" is the designation assigned to the queer character Gonzalo.

13. All English translations of *TransAtlantyk* come from Gombrowicz (1994).

14. According to Płonowska-Ziarek, for Gombrowicz "the 'in-between' position is more likely to be associated with creative energy when it is seen as a figure for textual experimentation alone; yet, when it refers explicitly to homosexual practices, it is all too often linked in homophobic culture with monstrosity, degeneration, and fear. Nonetheless, the transitivity of sexual identities in Gombrowicz's work also opens a possibility of intervention as it implies that the valorization of same-sex desire can be changed in different cultural sites" (1998a, 19).

15. See also Geneviève Zubrzycki (2007). "That narrative was forcefully created in the nineteenth century by Romantic poets who equated the Partitions of Poland with its crucifixion. Poland, in these writings, was the Christ of nations: sacrificed for the sins of the world, and it would be brought back to life to save humanity from absolutism" (119).

16. I wish to make it clear that this is not one of Joep Leersen's claims, but rather one of the misguided assumptions that helped lead to the rise of nationalism.

17. Andrzej Wajda focuses particularly on this dynamic in his 1999 film version of *Pan Tadeusz*. The film ends with the many Poles dancing the Polonaise off of the estate into a pasture, which then immediately cuts to the same Poles living in exile in France.

18. For an excellent queer analysis of *Ferdydurke*, see Kaliściak's (2016) chapter "Gombrowicz od tyłu. Project krytyki analnej na przykładzie powieści *Ferdydurke*" (pp. 170–222).

Chapter Two

Julian Stryjkowski

The Pole, the Jew, the Queer

By simply revealing the necessary violence inherent in normative regimes, both *TransAtlantyk* and *The Teacher* play a vital role in undermining such systems of power. Arguably, Gombrowicz's biting satire goes further in subverting traditional, heteronormative Polish values than Iwaszkiewicz's realism. However, ultimately the primary aim of both texts is to criticize conservative, reactionary principles that demand conformity to a prescribed morality, illustrating the dissident power of queer transgressive literature. In somewhat of a contrast to Gombrowicz's and Iwaszkiewicz's critical projects stands the more reconciliatory project of Julian Stryjkowski.[1]

The life-long struggle Stryjkowski faced as a Polish Jew to reconcile his Polishness with his Jewishness was made more complicated by both his devotion to communism as well as his queer sexuality. Grażyna Borkowska suggests that Stryjkowski practiced a selective method of self-definition, accepting the best of the Polish and Jewish, and rejecting the worse. She states, "It was not just a matter of answering the question, Jew or Pole? Stryjkowski knew very well that there existed many variants of Jewishness and Polishness. [. . .] He learned to accept and reject" (2002, 56–57). This idea of forming an identity through a kind of selective dialectics is certainly interesting; however, I would suggest, on the contrary, that ultimately Stryjkowski's life and work illustrate a conviction that there is no selection to be made. His work is transgressive, subverting received notions of what it means to be Polish, Jewish, queer, or Communist. It is ultimately a reconciliatory act that embraces the heterogeneous, and becomes a defiant stand against nationalist, normative ideologies that demand homogeneous modes of identification. The three works I analyze in this chapter, *In the Willows . . .*

Our Fiddles (1974) (*Na Wierzbach . . . Nasze Skrzypce*), *Tomasso del Cavielere* (1982), and his final published work of fiction, *Silence* (1993) (*Milczenie*) reveal a rejection of what he sees as the false choice between being Polish and being Jewish, a refusal to see them as mutually exclusive identities.[2]

Stryjkowski was born Pesach Stark in 1905 in the shtetl of Stryj in what was then Austrian-controlled eastern Galicia. He took the pseudonym Stryjkowski when he fled to the Soviet Union from the invading Nazis. Ireneusz Piekarski suggests that this early name change signals the beginning of Stryjkowski's questioning of "identity and its loss," which is "not only an existential problem but also an intratextual one—a very frequent and important motif in his writings" (2010, 308). His life was marked by paradoxical extremes. He grew up in a religiously Orthodox home, but went to a Polish school. He began his studies in Hebrew, but switched to Polish. At the age of twelve he ran away from home to join the Zionist organization Hashomer Hatzair, then later became a member of the Communist Party of Western Ukraine. From the end of the war until 1966 he was a member of the Polish United Workers' Party, only leaving in protest due to the expulsion of Leszek Kołakowski. As a young man, he refused to say kaddish at his father's funeral because of his communist beliefs—a moment he revisits fictionally in several of his works. He spent the war in Moscow, where he heard of the destruction of the Warsaw ghetto, and immediately began writing his first important work *Voices in the Dark* (1946).[3] Before this, according to Piekarski, Stryjkowski's works were "totally devoid of the Jewish element and [were] written purely from the Polish perspective" (309). Thereafter, most of Stryjkowski's writings, especially his so-called "Galician Tetralogy" become an attempt to memorialize the lost Jewish community of Poland, often being referred to as an epitaph or "headstone" over it (Polonsky and Adamczyk-Garbowska 2001, xiii). Antony Polonsky and Monika Adamczyk-Garbowska describe him as someone "who became a writer because of the tragic events of the war, the indirect chronicler of the Shoah, and the last guardian of the vast Jewish cemetery into which Poland was transformed" (1). Yet despite his concern about the destruction of Jewish Poland, he refused the many appeals of family and friends to move to Israel. Adamczyk-Garbowska rightly notes that "despite his consciousness of his Jewish roots" he would never be able to find his place in Israel. "He realize[d] that he w[ould] always be a stranger there, since the society of the Promised Land seem[ed] to be as intolerant of his difference as the society in Poland" (1998, 396).

Not only Stryjkowski's life but also his work illustrates this refusal to choose between his Polish and Jewish identities. According to Laura Quercioli Mincer, he suffered from an "internal schism" that originated from choosing "as his own, the language of the country in which he live[d]," which led to denying himself "any real means of dialogue either with his own community of origin or with the surrounding non-Jewish environment" (2001, 492). Despite this, he stubbornly clung to the hybrid identity he inhabited as a Polish Jew, and the struggles he faced because of it become an important theme in his writing.

In 1974, Stryjkowski published his novel *In the Willows . . . Our Fiddles*,[4] which was written following his trip to the United States as a visiting author at the International Writing Program (IWP) at the University of Iowa in 1969. It is divided into three chapters, each of which function almost as independent short stories. The first chapter, "The Swell" takes place on a ship during a voyage from Europe to America, while the other two describe the narrator's life in Los Angeles, all of which closely resembles Stryjkowski's 1969 trip. It is an Odyssean story, beginning with his voyage to America, and ending on a plane during his return trip to Poland. Letters in his file at the IWP reveal that Stryjkowski was forced to travel by ship on the liner Batory since he lacked sufficient funds to travel by plane, and that he travelled from Iowa to Los Angeles while in America (1972b).[5] In an interview with Wiesław Kot, Stryjkowski called himself a "most autobiographical writer," saying, "I never write about things I have not directly experienced" (qtd. in Kot 1997, 67). This assertion, as well as the character of his writing, leads me to place much of his work, including those pieces I analyze here, firmly within the genre of autofiction.[6] Not only does he write what he knows, but also what he writes is always very personal and often reflects his life, though obviously somewhat fictionalized.[7] The autofictional mode provides Stryjkowski a strategy through which he can more directly address personal subjects, and yet at the same time distance himself from them when necessary. In communist Poland of the 1970s it would have often been necessary for him to be able to maintain this distance. As Ewa Chudoba notes, Stryjkowski, "similarly to all other homosexual literati was being watched by the authorities" (2012, 216). While homosexuality was not officially illegal at the time, being publicly outed as gay would have had severe consequences both personally and professionally.

"The Swell" takes place almost entirely on a cross-Atlantic sea voyage. The setting of the ship stresses an in-betweenness, the voyage itself being a liminal space, and when the swell hits, it literally also becomes an unstable space. The rough seas make the narrator violently seasick, causing him to hallucinate. For several pages, the story moves between his fevered description of the illness, memories of his childhood, and thoughts about the Holocaust. This passage begins with a kind of confession when the narrator says, "I've survived so many terrible moments, I was always able to escape, though in the depths of my soul I was always ashamed to run away" (1974, 11–12). Struggling to the sink he sees his pale face in the mirror and it reminds him of a "Purim mask." "With my last effort I open the faucet, with one hand I wash my face, someone once told me that the first to die in the camps were the ones who stopped shaving" (14). Throughout the volume, Stryjkowski constantly returns to these feelings of guilt as a survivor, the narrator repeatedly facing contempt from either himself or from other characters.

This guilt is punctuated in "The Swell" with memories and hallucinatory dreams of escape. In one dream-memory the narrator describes how "there appeared the mask of my mother's distorted face beside my father running from dogs, his gabardine whipping in the wind. And I heard a scream: '*Jude! Jude!*' My father's face was smeared with blood like an Indian's" (13). With the use of the German "*Jude*," instead of the Polish "*Żyd*," one's thoughts immediately lead to a reading of this scene as the narrator and his family escaping from the Nazis during the Holocaust. The autofictitious plays an interesting role here as Stryjkowski himself was lucky enough to have avoided such an experience, escaping first to Ukraine and later to Moscow immediately following the beginning of the war. Allowing myself minimal use of his biography, I would suggest a different reading. Stryjkowski may very well be making a subtle comment against the communist authorities of Poland at the time. Following the Arab-Israeli Six Day War of 1967, during which the Soviet Union and its satellite states supported the Arab nations, there were mass expulsions of Jews from high-ranking positions in the communist parties of the Eastern Bloc. In Poland, the regime-supported "Anti-Zionist" campaign of March 1968 would eventually see the exit of most of the remaining 50,000 Polish Jews first from the party, if they were members, and later from the country. This episode could be read as a moment of Stryjkowski making use of his biography to accomplish several things. First, he highlights the Jewish identity of the narrator, who to some degree—however small—is a stand-in for Stryjkowski himself. Secondly, this dream-memory, in connection with his previous expression of shame, adds to discussions of the phenomenon of survivor guilt. Finally, the narrator's dream-memory could very well function as a metaphor of the anti-Jewish campaign of 1967 and 1968.[8] It does not seem to be a coincidence that Stryjkowski travelled out of the communist sphere, and stayed away for as long as he did, so soon after the anti-Semitic actions of the previous year.

Later, the narrator describes another dream of escape that is tied more closely to his feelings of guilt for having survived the Holocaust:

> I'm running, they chase, I'm barefoot. I hold on to an apple with all my strength [. . .] a priest runs after me with a stick in his hand. [. . .] Here Gestapo men with dogs on leashes are waiting, pointing at me: "*Jude, komm!*" I feel that I am naked, around my neck hangs a copper cross, I raise it to my lips and scream the words of a prayer. [. . .] I'm running, everyone runs after me, the entire village where my grandparents live, my father's parents, my father chases after me on the burning wings of his gabardine, I jump into the water. I drown. (15)

The image of the narrator being persecuted for such a minor offense as stealing an apple from an orchard implies that he is actually being punished simply for being a Jew. This becomes more apparent when instead of a priest he suddenly finds himself harassed by the Gestapo. The apple references the story of Genesis, his theft of it implying the original sin of Adam and Eve. Here, however, the narrator's original sin is being born a Jew. The passage turns on the moment he says a prayer on a copper cross he suddenly finds hanging from his neck. In an act of self-preservation, he converts to Christianity. Though this act saves him from the priest and the Nazis, it turns his own people against him. Being rejected by both worlds his only escape, finally, is death. This theme of estrangement runs throughout Stryjkowski's works, reflecting his constant struggle with maintaining his hybrid identity as a Polish Jew.

The theft of fruit also brings to mind Book II of Saint Augustine's *Confessions*, in which he steals pears from an orchard:

> For I stole that, of which I had enough, and much better. Nor cared I to enjoy what I stole, but joyed in the theft and sin itself. [. . .] And this but to do, what we liked only, because it was misliked. Behold my heart, O God, behold my heart, which Thou hadst pity upon in the bottom of the bottomless pit. (25–26)

Through the recognition of his guilt and confession of his sin, Augustine has prepared himself for God's grace. It is a moment that leads him to salvation. For Stryjkowski's narrator, the theft of fruit also leads to a Christian salvation; however, instead of achieving some kind of positive affirmation, the act leads to feelings of guilt for having betrayed his own people.[9]

Stryjkowski highlights this sense of estrangement in several later passages in the chapter when the narrator refuses to be honest when telling people any details about himself. At one point the narrator's cabinmate convinces him to drink "*bruderschaft*," a Polish tradition in which two people move from using the formal mode of address to the informal. The cabinmate tells him his name is Edek, to which the narrator replies "Dawid." Later we will learn that his real name is Leon. Seeming to understand that the narrator has not given his true name, Edek replies, "Ok, fine. It's all the same to me" (28). That he uses a false name is especially telling, as it follows the *bruderschaft* ceremony. Participants in this are expected to provide their real names, to reveal their true identities, an act that creates a mutual vulnerability between the two. However, not only does the narrator refuse to do this, he continues the lie when he tells Edek that he is on his way to Moline, Illinois, to work in the John Deere tractor factory, which is actually a repetition of something other characters had told him about earlier in the story. His lies become even more absurd in a later conversation when he tells a character that he is a silkworm farmer. The volatile, liminal space of the ocean not only literally destabilizes the narrator, who remains unnamed in the first chapter, it also undermines the borders of his self, creating an opportunity for him to play with his identity. This play reveals Stryjkowski's interest in and desire for malleable, fluid modes of identification and a resistance to ideologies that work to limit and concretize identity. In *The Location of Culture*, Homi Bhabha describes in-between spaces as the most productive areas of "selfhood," which "initiate new signs of identity" (1994, 1). During his transatlantic journey, the narrator takes advantage of this interstitial moment to do just that. It is an act reminiscent of Gombrowicz-the-character in *TransAtlantyk*, who also takes advantage of the "in-between-ness" of a cross-Atlantic voyage to re-define himself.

The chapter ends with a memory/dream of the narrator as a young boy riding in a cart beside his mother. As they come into view of a village his mother tells him, "There is our town, there, there, our village" (42). It is a strange ending to the first part of a text about journey; it begins the narrator's story, a story about travelling half-way around the world, with a desire to return home. Of course, the return is impossible, since it is a home that has not existed for over thirty years. The chapter "The Swell," the most surreal of the three, introduces themes the narrator will continue to struggle with—the wish to return to a lost home, the guilt of being a survivor, and a desire for a fluid, ambiguous identity.

The second chapter of the novel is "Sirius," the title of which comes from a scene in the story when the narrator and his niece stop at the side of the Los Angeles freeway to look at the stars. He looks for Sirius, the brightest star, which makes up part of the constellation Canis Major. When he cannot find it, he says, "I understood what it meant to be a stranger everywhere" (80). This is a powerful statement about the narrator's experience. It is not simply that in America he views himself as an outsider; he feels like an outsider everywhere, including in his homeland, a sentiment that undoubtedly reflects Stryjkowski's own experiences.

The chapter takes place in Los Angeles months after the narrator's arrival in America. Now finally named Leon, he arrives in Los Angeles to visit his niece and her family. A tension immediately arises when his grandniece inexplicably protests her mother and Leon speaking Polish, saying she does not like the language, although she understands and speaks it herself. From the very beginning of the story his Polishness is rejected by the caprice of a child. Though most of the other characters speak Polish, throughout the rest of the story the narrator will speak only English or Yiddish. This rejection of his Polish identity by others is repeated several times in the chapter, as various characters reply with incredulity when he refuses to stay in America, and instead plans to return to communist Poland.

Leon's plans with his niece are suddenly interrupted when an old friend, Nysen, from the same shtetl in Poland, appears and convinces him to come to a dinner party at his house. On the way, Leon and Nysen reminisce about their childhood. Leon tells Nysen that nothing is left of their village; the Jewish cemetery has disappeared, and the town square is overgrown with grass. He says, "There was a town, there were people and the next moment everything had disappeared. There's nothing. Simply nothing. Torn from the Earth" (79). Leon's description of Nysen's affluent gated community and luxurious mansion presents a vivid contrast to the devastation of Jewish life in Poland.

The scene of the dinner party further highlights Leon's feelings of estrangement and isolation. Within the group are several old friends from Poland before the war. Despite their common past, he is unable to relate to them in the context of their newfound lives in America. As Paweł Śpiewak rightly points out, Leon's meeting "with the American Jewish community strongly underlines the border between him and the others" (1974, 101). At one point, they ask him to say something to the group:

> "What can I say?" I reflected, as if I really wanted to make a declaration that from the first moment they had been expecting from me. . . . The seconds passed in silence. I dried the sweat on my forehead with my handkerchief.
> "My dear friends," I began, "I have nothing to say to you."
> The guests looked at each other and returned to their dinner. (177)

From the moment Leon joined them, the guests had been praising their life in America. Now they also expect him to extoll America and the prosperity they have found there. However, Leon is unimpressed, and indeed rather appalled by the community's extravagance. His inability to speak here is a reflection of his inability to identify with this community. Though also a Jew, he cannot recognize himself within this iteration of Jewish life. Polonsky and Adamczyk-Garbowska read this scene as Stryjkowski finding his "encounter with American Jewish life [. . .] disconcerting [. . .]. [He] felt unable to communicate his own Jewish experience" (2001, xxxii). The disconnection Leon experiences with the American Jewish community is a product of both his desire to remain Polish as well as his communist sympathies. The other guests find it strange and incomprehensible that the narrator refuses to even consider leaving Poland. For Leon, it is a refusal to abandon part of an identity he had struggled to make his own. As Adamczyk-Garbowska puts it, "Emigration to America would deprive him of his frames of reference, and it would not bring him closer to his Jewish roots, because Jewish tradition in its Californian version seems to him like a parody of the old way of life" (2008, 629). Like Stryjkowski, the narrator is a member of the Communist Party. Although Stryjkowski eventually did leave the Party, he remained a believer in communism, never apologizing for his affiliation with it. Similarly, Leon, as a communist, is disturbed by the bourgeois life in which he finds the community he once called his own.

The narrator also seems to be critical of what he understands to be an "ersatz shtetl" nestled in the Hollywood hills. Though it is a community inhabited by many of the same people as before, Leon views it as little more than a simulacrum, a base copy of the life they had known in Poland. The rabbi, an old friend of his, has changed his name from Jakub Stein to Jack Stone, and has married a gentile. There is even a character taking on the role of the village fool, though unable to impart wisdom or any deeper insights from his foolishness. Most distressing for Leon is that conspicuous consumption has taken the place of communal living. Harriet Murav notes that for Soviet Jewish authors, "The shtetl was both the holy city and the place where the Jewish body politic had its existence, [. . .] its foundation was linked to a transcendental intervention that vouchsafed its continuity with Jewish sacred history; and finally it was a temporary home for the Jewish people, who would ultimately be restored to Israel" (2011, 249). Leon, however, is unable to find the same possibilities in the American example. He realizes that the shtetl that had been "torn from the Earth" has not been replaced here, despite the efforts of the inhabitants.

The tensions Stryjkowski describes between Leon and the American Jewish community over Leon's desire to maintain his Polishness contrast with his celebration of his Jewishness in the final chapter of the novel, the titular "In the Willows . . . Our Fiddles." Leon is working as a visiting professor at a university in California; it is never made clear which. In one scene, he goes to a vocal performance concert by a Hasidic rabbi. He is surprised when he first hears of the concert, saying,

> I had to travel across the Atlantic to see a piece of a lost world. There no longer were any true Hasidim in worn gabardines, wearing shabby caps, wandering the streets like shadows, with a halo of passion over their heads, a fog of ignorance for earthly fear in their eyes. (156)

Again, Stryjkowski's narrator mourns the lost home and the impossibility of return. It is a surreal moment, since in order once again to experience the Old World he must travel to the New World. As he listens to the rabbi sing, he reflects that "such a clear tone I only heard once in my life and I had longed for it, though in vain. It would never repeat itself, and perhaps it had never been, and I had only dreamed it in a forgotten dream" (175). So far from the lost world in which he had last heard such music, the narrator revels in its beauty. Unlike in the previous chapter where he lamented the pale replication of the shtetl, here he experiences a kind of return to that lost home. Though he continues to feel isolated, at this moment he also feels a connection to the Jewish people, and he rejoices in it.

Important to an understanding of this chapter is an analysis of the title itself, which comes from the second line of Psalm 137, "By the rivers of Babylon." Curiously, that verse, "There in the willows we hung our harps," ends with the word "harps," not "fiddles." The word Stryjkowski uses in Polish is *"skrzypce*," which can be translated as either "fiddle" or "violin," but never "harp." The word *"harfy,"* "harps" appears in almost every Polish translation of the Bible. The *Brest Bible* of 1563, and the *Updated Gdańsk Bible* (*UBG*) of 1632, both use "harfy" in this line. One exception is the 1599 *Wujek Bible*, which uses the phrase *"muzyckie naczynia*" (musical instruments). Stryjkowski's use of "fiddles" in place of the more common "harps" leads me to make a comparison between his story and Chekhov's "Rothschild's Fiddle."[10] While I would not wish to delve into "influence" studies, or authorial intent, Stryjkowski would have undoubtedly been familiar with Chekhov. But whether or not Stryjkowski is making a purposeful connection to "Rothschild's Fiddle" is beside the point. In both stories, the fiddle—as a culturally significant object of Eastern European Jewish identity—acts as a mechanism for reconciliation between Jew and Gentile. In his analysis of "Rothschild's Fiddle," Robert Louis Jackson makes a connection between the story and Psalm 137, not only through direct allusions, but also especially in terms of the theme of repentance, noting the importance of the psalm and the figure of the "prodigal son" (2007, 202). In Chekhov's story, Iakov and Rothschild become reconciled when Iakov, distressed by the death of his wife, apologizes to Rothschild for his earlier abuse. He then bequeaths his fiddle to Rothschild before dying. In "Willows," Stryjkowski describes a similar moment of reconciliation. When the narrator attends the concert by the Hasidic rabbi, a young German named Nikolas accompanies him. When the rabbi begins singing Psalm 137, Nikolas asks the narrator to translate from the Hebrew for him. The dynamic that occurs between the narrator and Nikolas is remarkable. Within the text of Psalm 137 there appear the lines: "for there our captors asked us for songs, / our tormentors demanded songs of joy; / they said, 'Sing us one of the songs of Zion!'" When they first meet, Nikolas asks the narrator not to think badly of him for being a German, saying that his father was a minister who opposed the Nazis, even serving prison time for his opposition. From that point on, the Holocaust hangs over their budding friendship, and in the context of the psalm, Nikolas—as a German—is one of the "captors." However, the concert provides a power reversal between the two. The narrator is now in a position of authority over Nikolas, who does not understand the language. Just as when Iakov gives his fiddle to Rothschild the two reconcile, so too does the act of Stryjkowski's narrator translating for Nikolas operate as a gesture of reconciliation. It is also significant that the impetus behind this reconciliation is the attraction the two feel for each other.

In her essay "The Homelessness of the Other," Borkowska suggests that "homoeroticism is the key to understanding Stryjkowski's relation to the world," and is the central defining theme of *In the Willows* (2002, 61). While I agree with much of Borkowska's analysis of Stryjkowski's life and work, it is an exaggeration to suggest that the homoerotic is the "key" to understanding this work. There are no explicit expressions of homoerotic desire made by either Leon or any other character. Instead Stryjkowski punctuates the narrative with occasional hints at the truth of the narrator's desires. In the chapter "Sirius," for example, Leon is repeatedly asked about his wife and children. It is never a question as to whether he is married, but instead there is an assumption that he is obviously married. At one point when he replies that he is not married, his interlocutors assume that his wife and children died during the Holocaust. When he responds that he has never been married the reaction is one of astonishment. The dinner guests reveal their deep belief in a compulsory heterosexuality that seems foreign to Leon. Upon seeing Jakub Stein—the rabbi who had changed his name to Jack Stone having moved to the United States—again after so many years, Leon thinks, "Jakub's gloomy, closed face still seemed both beautiful and terrible like in times past when we were united by an inseparable friendship" (101). For several pages, the two have an impassioned argument about their shared past, but it is fragmentary, punctuated by incomplete sentences that only they can understand. Leon recounts a fight the two had: "You attacked me in the grove. We were fighting, you threw me to the ground, you were stronger than I. I had to bite your chest" (102). The reason for their fight is never made explicit, but Leon's biting of Jakub's chest might insinuate a deep passion as it symbolically replaces a kiss. This passion seems to be confirmed later when Leon tells Jakub, "I loved you" (103). The conversation continues, again interspersed with silences. At the end of their conversation Jakub begins to say, "If you'd married . . . ," but before he can finish, Leon replies curtly "Bah!" (135). While the silences and unfinished statements between Leon and Jakub certainly do suggest an erotic connection between the two, I would hesitate to suggest that it is the "key" to understanding the novel. Rather, the inexpressible desires between them are yet another layer of the narrator's struggle with his competing identities, being a Pole, a Jew, a communist, as well as a gay man.

The chapter "In the Willows" is similarly ambiguous on the subject of the narrator's desires. The story begins with Leon receiving a call from a woman he had known during his teenage years in Poland. The phone call is followed by a long passage in which the narrator recalls their relationship. As a girl, Fela had been an object of attraction for all the town's boys, except for the narrator. At one point, he remembers watching a film when Fela and his friend Szymek come and sit down next to him. Fela suddenly leans over and kisses his ear, which he finds extremely unpleasant and leads to him having a nightmare: "I was awoken by my own scream, when in the dream Fela sat on me, straddling my chest" (150). This fear of being dominated by a woman further reveals his distaste for the hetero-erotic. This is highlighted again when he recalls catching Fela and Szymek naked on a couch, asleep post coitus:

> I covered my mouth with my hand. I couldn't move, I stood and looked, I shook and looked. My face burned. I do not remember how I got out of there, or how I returned home. Whether I went on my own or if someone took me. Maybe I fell on the doorstep and they took me while I was unconscious. After a few days, I rose as from a terrible sickness. No one ever asked me about it. No one ever discovered why I had fainted. No one ever reminded me of it and even I forgot about it. (152)

More than mere modesty, this passage reveals a near revulsion at female sexuality, so much so that the narrator must repress it from his memories. This revulsion is described further in a later passage when a drunken female student who wants him to seduce her visits the narrator. She undresses and attempts to make him kiss a copper cross hanging between her breasts. This reappearance of the copper cross, of course, leads the reader back to the narrator's nightmare at the beginning of the novel, when he symbolically accepts it and converts. This time, however, now that the cross is connected erotically with a woman, he refuses to accept it, and quickly leaves the room. His shock and utter inability to deal with the situation, combined with the earlier fainting scene, illustrate his complete disinterest in women.

The sudden friendship between the narrator and Nikolas also insinuates an element of homoerotic desire. Like Leon's discussion with Jakub, the conversation between the narrator and Nikolas is full of things half said, with never more than hints at their attraction to each other. At one point, they come across a nude couple leaving a pool. Nikolas tries to convince the narrator to go for a swim with him "completely naked. As the Lord God created us." When Nikolas asks why he is quiet Leon replies, "because that is not for me," to which Nikolas replies with an ambiguous, "Perhaps" (170). The narrator says nothing in reply. Once again there is only silence in the face of queer desire. Here, similarly to Iwaszkiewicz in *The Teacher*, Stryjkowski makes use of ambiguity, illustrating again Sedgwick's observation that male homoerotic desire must maintain "a precisely liminal presence," relying on a "thematics of absence, and specifically of the absence of speech" (1990, 201). Especially in the context of communist Poland of the 1970s, when any literary expression of the homoerotic would have been nearly impossible to express freely, the narrator's desire for Nikolas can only be intimated in these "absences of speech." Despite his unwillingness to join Nikolas in skinny-dipping, their friendship continues, culminating when they tell each other "I like you" near the end of the novel. For readers looking back at the text forty years later, knowing more about Stryjkowski's "homobiography," the desire Nikolas and Leon feel for each other seems obvious. However, it must be admitted that the expression of this desire is highly sublimated, locked in silences that general readers in Poland in 1974 very likely would not have been able to decipher, nor would they have wanted to.

The key theme of the novel, more so than homoeroticism, is that of the estrangement brought about by Leon's struggle with his Polish/Jewish/communist identity, a struggle that is certainly complicated further by his queer desires. Polonsky and Adamczyk-Garbowska describe Stryjkowski as, "a man marked by difference. He felt estranged in Poland because of his Jewish origins, and because his language was Polish he was also a stranger in Israel and the Jewish communities of America. Finally, he felt difference because of his homosexuality" (2008, xv). All three chapters highlight an overwhelming sense of isolation. In "The Swell" the narrator is unable to connect personally with other people. However, the setting of the story, the literally unstable space of the ocean, acts as a catalyst for the narrator to play with his identity, which in the end illustrates a kind of empowerment through his alienation. These themes continue in the chapter "Sirius," when Leon finds it impossible to relate to the American Jewish community. His refusal to sacrifice any part of his identity for another is a powerful act of self-definition, but one that denies him a close bond with a community he still wishes to consider his own. Otherness becomes a force for reconciliation in the chapter "In the Willows . . . Our Fiddles." Leon's "in-between" national/ethnic identity, coupled with his transgressive desires, allows him to become an intermediary between two cultures. Ultimately, Stryjkowski's novel reveals the ability for alterity to function as a productive force.

Stryjkowski's novella *Tommaso del Cavaliere*, published in 1982, is his first work that could truly be said to explicitly discuss homoerotic desire. It tells the story of the last days in the life of Michelangelo. Like much of Stryjkowski's other fiction, it is written in the first person, told by a narrator who remains unnamed. The narrator reveals almost nothing about himself. The few details that do appear are always in the context of his interaction with Michelangelo. I read this nebulous character of the narrator as a function of the autofictitious, allowing him to act as a stand-in for Stryjkowski though in a different time and place. Much of the story consists of reflections by the narrator on the relationship between Michelangelo and his lover Tommaso del Cavaliere. In a conversation between the two early in their friendship, the narrator describes Michelangelo telling del Cavaliere, "do not be afraid of nudity. God created us naked, and thus gave us the perfect shape. Nudity is Beauty. Nudity is the truth of art" (15). Michelangelo's defense of nudity, especially male nudity, becomes a recurring theme in the novella as he must continually defend his sculptures to the church authorities who wish to cover their genitalia. The narrator also describes carrying gifts from Michelangelo to del Cavaliere, and letters between them. In looking over the paintings Michelangelo sends the young man, the narrator wonders about the symbolism, whether there are "allusions to the passion of love," or perhaps they describe "a hotbed of desire" (12). Later the narrator describes an argument between Michelangelo and another character over physical love. When the character states that "when [Socrates] thought about love, he was not thinking about carnal pleasures," Michelangelo curtly replies, "I don't believe it" (15). Similarly to the references of Ancient Greece in *The Teacher*, this reference to Socrates and his thoughts on love, again evoke Plato's *Symposium* and Pausanias's discussion on the sublimity of the love between men (1994, 13–19). In contrast to his earlier *In the Willows*, here Stryjkowski has begun a more open discussion of the homoerotic, though couched in a story that takes place several centuries earlier.

This temporal setting itself is of fundamental importance to the narrative. Unlike his other fiction, most of which takes place during his own lifetime, or, in the case of his biblical trilogy, is at least concerned with the theme of Judaic history, *del Cavaliere* is set 500 years prior, and Judaism plays no role whatsoever. His choice of setting appears quite deliberate, since it provided Stryjkowski with a necessary distance between himself and the topic of gay male love, especially in the Poland of the 1980s. Between 1981 and 1983, martial law was in place in Poland. Though introduced in an attempt to suppress the trade union Solidarity, the authorities used martial law to target anyone they deemed counter-revolutionary, including the Polish gay community. One such documented case was Operation Hyacinth. The police and national militia raided gay clubs and the homes of gay people, rounded many of them up, and interrogated them. Within this context, *del Cavaliere* is a truly daring work. It is much more openly homoerotic than Stryjkowski's prior writing precisely because it cannot be directly connected to his autobiography. Stryjkowski was able to find a way to broach the topic of gay desire in the midst of the largest anti-gay crackdown in Polish history. Though many see his final work, *Silence,* as his "coming-out" piece, *del Cavaliere* is actually a much more open work about non-normative desire.

Stryjkowski's clearest struggle between his competing identities appears in *Silence*, which was published in 1993, just three years before his death. By compounding his Polish Jewish "nationality" with his queer sexuality, the novella disrupts notions of stable, unitary modes of national and gendered identification. The story is told as a memoir, the eighty-year-old narrator reflecting on his life as a gay Polish Jew, having been a Zionist and then communist in early twentieth-century Poland. Although, as in many of his other stories the narrator remains unnamed, it is clear that this is one of Stryjkowski's most autobiographical works. In 1994, he said of his novella and of the subject of his sexuality,

> I attacked this theme several times before. I never before did it frontally. I tore off the veil only in *Milczenie*. I thought to myself, "You are eighty years old." Write it, let it be your last book, slam the door shut, let there be no more of your words, write nothing more about anything. (qtd. in Kot 1997, 143).

Though with this novella Stryjkowski wished to "tear off the veil" about his sexuality, the methods he uses to discuss it are highly ambiguous. This ambiguity is mixed with the memoir style that firmly places this work in the autofiction genre. Until the final pages of the novella, the reader is provided only hints and innuendo as to the subject of the narrator being gay. Indeed, rather than opening the story with a clear statement about his desires, he begins instead with an indictment of nationalism and nationalist movements:

> Who today is fascinated by Vladimir Zhabotinskii?[11] Who today cares about the squads of Jewish boys and girls marching down Jewish streets dressed in brown shirts like the Hitlerjugend, still unstructured and mild, but already seething with the menace of a predator? (1993, 5)

It is a daring opening. On the surface, he seems to equate the Jewish nationalist defense movements of the early twentieth century with the National Socialist movement of fascist Germany. However, he softens the comparison when he calls the marching Jewish youth "unstructured and mild," demonstrating his understanding that there cannot be a one-to-one correlation between them and the Hitler Youth. Certainly, the narrator denounces Jewish nationalism by implying the comparison, but in fact the narrative suggests a broader condemnation of nationalism writ large.

The narrator elaborates on this comparison through a description of two of his school friends. The first is Oskar Wagner, who goes back to Germany, his homeland, post-graduation. Though he was German, Wagner "never displayed it"; however, he later returns "with the Hakenkreuz [or Swastika] under his lapel, like a spy." Wagner then tries to convince the Jewish narrator, "that Hitler, only Hitler . . . Stalin wants to rule the world but Hitler will not let him, and he will save humanity" (5–6). Although the narrator had considered him a friend while he was not "displaying" his Germanness, he labels Wagner a "spy" when he returns espousing his support for the Nazi movement. This friendship is immediately contrasted with the narrator's friendship with Jakub Wald, who, after school, leaves for Palestine. The narrator's description of Wald's motives makes a clear comparison with those of Wagner's: "In order to fight the Arabs, and also to defeat Hitler, he put on a brown shirt, the color of which was a not entirely Nazi brown, and illegally emigrated to Erets, as the biblical homeland was called" (6). Like Wagner, Wald also leaves the heterogeneous homeland of the eastern Polish *Kresy* for a mythically homogenous ur-homeland. In his description of Wald putting on a not quite Nazi brown shirt, the narrator implies that both Wagner and Wald represent systems of nationalism, systems he finds constrictive and oppressive. What separates Wagner and Wald is the difference in degree of affection the narrator expresses for them. While there is not another mention of Wagner throughout the rest of the novella, Jakub remains an important figure. Indeed, the narrator's rivalry with Jakub, and his struggle with his desire for him, becomes the central theme of the story.

Silence functions as a two-fold "coming-out" story. Not only is it the first work in which Stryjkowski, through his fictionalized narrator, speaks somewhat openly about his sexuality and his struggles with coming to terms with it, it also reveals that, even at the age of eighty-eight, he remained unapologetically nostalgic about the communist ideals of his youth. In 1952, his expression of these ideals even got him expelled from Italy, where he was the director of the Polish Press Agency (PAP). This occurred with the publication of his novel *Race to Fragal*, which describes the struggles of peasants in Calabria (Mincer 2001, 494). *Silence* becomes another political work expressing Stryjkowski's fervent anti-nationalism. It would be easy to suggest that what the anti-Jewish nationalist passages reveal is a kind of self-hating anti-Semitism. However, one must take into account that they were written by the same author who spent most of his creative efforts writing about and mourning the lost Jewish world of Central and Eastern Europe. Instead, I read these opening pages as an expression of Stryjkowski's distrust of any nationalist movement that seeks a homogenous, unitary state, his communist identity further complicating his Polish-Jewish-Queer identification.

After waiting for word from Jakub following his arrival in Palestine, the narrator finally writes to him: "And then I wrote a letter to him in ostentatious Polish. It was a sign that our paths had divided" (7). Though, like Stryjkowski, he knows Hebrew, the narrator purposely uses a highly stylized Polish to communicate with Jakub. In choosing Polish, he claims a right to his Polish identity, an act directed not only toward Jews who question his authenticity as a Jew, but also toward non-Jewish Poles who question his assertion of Polishness. In his letter he tells Jakub, "You've become a Jewish fascist, and I went to the side of communism" (7). He again compares the brown shirts of the Israeli youth to those of the Hitler Youth, and says that as communists, "we have on our side a just picture of the world. It fills me with pride that I can say that" (8). For the narrator, the simple act of writing in Polish illustrates the division between himself and Jakub, but what makes their separation truly definitive is politics. He continues the letter:

> I have no desire to spread the plague in Granada. However, I am counting on your discretion. Perhaps on account of our dualistic friendship you will not want me packed off to prison. Many things you know how to do well, but you are best at staying quiet. [. . .] The respect you garnered weighed heavily [. . .]. I don't have it. This is why I feel your contempt—I exaggerate—your disap-

proval, which you have for any weakness. Is this perhaps the root of your fascism? (8)

The letter begins the theme of silence central to the novella. The narrator's attacks on Jakub are vague and elliptical, practically indecipherable for the reader. He uses the esoteric reference to the practice of blaming the Jewish community of medieval Spain for spreading the plague as a metaphor for rumor, and speaks of "discretion" and their "dualistic friendship." He suggests that Jakub knows of some secret that could have him "packed off to prison," but what that secret might be he never makes clear. The narrator tells Jakub that what he knows how to do best is "*milczeć*" or "stay quiet." The accusation is that in the past the narrator needed Jakub to say something, but did not. He then mentions some "weakness" he has, of which Jakub disapproves, wondering whether it is the cause of Jakub's "fascism." Again, though his accusations are highly emotional, and clearly stem from the narrator and Jakub's mutual past, their true cause remains pointedly ambiguous. In the context of the rest of the story one could infer that the narrator's letter is related to an intimate past the two shared. However, if *Silence* was supposed to be, as Stryjkowski called it, a "frontal attack," a "tearing off the veil" from his gay identity, it is strange that he would address it in such an ambiguous manner. The necessity for him to keep his desires secret at the time the letter was written—that is, during his youth in Soviet Ukraine—is due to the fact that homosexuality was then illegal in the USSR. As Małgorzata Sadowska states, "Stryjkowski, who was able to escape the Holocaust, found himself in a different trap—homosexuality was punishable in the USSR by several years in prison" (2001, 385). That he remains unable to address it unambiguously in *Silence*, written well after any concerns about the legality of his desires were moot, suggests that even in post-communist Poland, transgressing the homosocial/homosexual line remained a difficult challenge.

Jakub replies with a letter written in Hebrew—the narrator's "weakness." He writes, "your Polish letter isn't worth anything." Jakub accuses him "a second time, of no longer being a Jew. 'Communism [. . .] is worse than baptism'" (9). These accusations get to the heart of the narrator's own anxieties about his authenticity. Jakub rejects his use of Polish, calling it worthless, well aware that the Polish language, and the narrator's ability to use it creatively, are fundamental to his attempts at identity creation. But Jakub dismisses it out of hand. For him there exist true Jews and false Jews, and the narrator's Polishness and communism mark him as a false Jew. In *The Great Fear*, Stryjkowski states, "Polish communists, Russian communists, or French communists do not stop being Poles, Russians, or Frenchmen. Jewish communists stop being Jews because they have no nation of their own" (qtd. in Szewc 1984, 54). While deciding to become a communist has cut Stryjkowski and his narrator off from the Jewish community, their Jewishness prevents them from taking part in the Polish nation. Jakub's letter reveals that, as a Jew who wishes to hold on to his Jewish, Polish, and communist identities, not only must the narrator struggle with Polish nationalists, he must also defend his choices against Jewish nationalists. Like Stryjkowski, the narrator does not wish to abandon any of these identities for any other. He simply refuses to believe that there is any necessity to choose between them.

After these letters, there is very little mention of the narrator's communism. Instead the story begins focusing on his struggle with his gay identity. Again, though for most readers the scenes in which he describes this struggle are obvious, there is never a moment in which he openly states that he is gay. As in the letter to Jakub, these scenes maintain an element of ambiguity, a vagueness that speaks once again to the novella's theme of silence. In one telling, though rather parenthetical scene, the narrator describes a moment when, as a child, he "put on a dress and felt happy." His father yells at him, and the narrator says, "he knew everything" (19). That others "know" before one knows for him/herself is a common theme in coming-out literature. A similar scene is repeated near the end of the book when he visits Jakub years later in Israel. Jakub tells him, "I've known about you for a long time, since you were practically a child. And don't think that you were able to hide from others. People know everything, even if it seems to us that secrets actually exist" (65). As in the earlier scene with the narrator's father, Jakub has known about the narrator's desires. He also, again like the father, voices his disapproval of these desires, despite the narrator's attempts to repress them. One example that contrasts with his father's and Jakub's reactions takes place midway through the novella. The narrator, distraught over a hallucination he had of a naked woman pointing at him threateningly, visits a psychiatrist. His refusal to accept a prescription for a sleeping aid prompts the following conversation:

> "Until now none of my patients have ever reacted in such a way to a prescription. I've had a lot of patients with various disorders; perverts, buzerants."
>
> "What's a buzerant?"
>
> [...]
>
> "It's from Austria. In Vienna Buzer is a game where you play Billiards with the stick behind your back. You can probably guess what it's describing."
>
> "Of course. Interesting. What won't perverts think up?"
>
> The doctor looked at me with interest.
>
> "A buzerant, or in our language, homosexual, is no pervert. A person is born with it. It is his nature. And there is no medicine for it. No Freudian therapy will help. Sexual psychology in this case is charlatanism. [...] That a homosexual can defeat his nature is nonsense."
>
> "He can remain abstinent. After all, it seems to me that a pervert comes into the world with a curable disorder."

The doctor nodded his head. I wasn't sure if he agreed or simply pitied me. (42–43)

The hallucination of the naked woman threatening the narrator recalls scenes from *In the Willows*, such as Leon's nightmare of Fela suffocating him, his fainting at the site of her naked, and his distress over a female student attempting to seduce him. As in the earlier story, this horror and even revulsion toward female sexuality reveals his complete disinterest in women. The narrator's strong reaction to the explanation of the word "buzerant" informs the psychiatrist as to the true nature of his problem. He is attempting to hide behind denial and an expression of homophobia, both of which only make his desires more obvious to the doctor. In response, the psychiatrist tells him something that he had never heard anyone else say: your desires are perfectly natural.

This encounter becomes a turning point for the narrator and his journey to self-definition. Before his conversation with the psychiatrist he is always a passive participant in his erotic encounters with both men and women. Early in the story he describes lying on a beach when suddenly a man approaches him and asks him to put suntan lotion on his back. The narrator responds by going into the water, saying, "luckily, he didn't know how to swim well" (17). Instead of confronting the man and his advances, the narrator avoids the encounter altogether. In a later scene he visits Marian, a young pianist. After some drinks, Marian begins rubbing his leg. "I grabbed it [Marian's hand] with two fingers and placed it on the plush couch. Marian stood and went to the window. He said in an uneasy voice: 'You're a hypocrite to your very marrow'" (26). The narrator then immediately leaves. He had not found himself in the apartment drunk and alone with Marian by accident. He had made the conscious decision to come to Marian's by himself. Despite this, he cannot succumb to his desires for Marian, still holding on to the belief that those desires are deviant, and that he can instead remain abstinent as he later suggests to the psychiatrist. Following this scene, the narrator describes one of his failed attempts at romance with women. He meets the character Maryla at a park and gives her flowers. She tries to be affectionate with him, but he is uncomfortable with the situation:

> She held me around my neck and whispered: "Well say it." I died. "You bought me these roses. You want to tell me something. . . . Well. . . . Well. . . . What's wrong?"
>
> This is senseless. This is the last time I play the seducer, or rather the seduced.
>
> I try and try, until I'm exhausted. But I won't be cornered. I could even get married. But with open doors. For both. Asylum and an end of this torment. Without the yoke of love. God! How miserable this is! (29)

Before meeting Maryla, the narrator describes preparing to bring her back to his room, going so far as to convince his roommate to leave for the night. However, as soon as she shows her receptivity to his advances he hesitates. As in the previous scene with Marian, though he has purposefully found himself in a romantic situation, the narrator remains unable to act due to his passivity. He is even uncertain whether he is acting as the seducer or the seduced. He finally gives voice to his distress, however, even suggesting that marriage, "without love" might be an answer.

After his conversation with the psychiatrist, however, the narrator has a final, more active encounter with both Maryla and Marian. He says, "I decided to propose to Maryla" (47). That he "decides" is itself an act that, before his meeting with the psychiatrist, was nearly impossible for him. To propose he plans on giving her a copy of one of his new books of poems with a dedication asking for her hand. Though he is now able to take on a more active role in his romantic life, he remains able to express it only indirectly. He asks her to read the dedication aloud. But instead, "Maryla laughed. 'You want me to propose to myself and to ask myself for my own hand. You know how to write what you cannot simply say. My poor poet! Do you really want to marry me?'" (48–49). He does not answer her, and their conversation ends without a true conclusion. Immediately following his failed proposal, he finds an invitation from Marian to his home to say goodbye before he leaves on a trip. He hurries to Marian's, but finds him almost ready to leave. All they are able to do is drink to one another's health before Marian whispers in his ear, "Think about me. [. . .] I'll write" (53–54). The urgency the narrator describes in his hurry to see Marian reveals his resolution to finally do something about his desires. However, as in the previous scene with Maryla, this encounter, too, ends without any fulfillment. It is no accident that the names of the two people with whom he comes closest to some kind of consummation are so similar. Anna Sobolewska suggests that Marian and Maryla are doppelgangers (2003, 39). For Stryjkowski they are essentially the same person manifested in both genders. At this point in the story, love with either a man or a woman is impossible for the narrator. And though his relationships with Marian and Maryla ultimately fail romantically, even after his visit to the psychiatrist, the narrator has finally realized a degree of agency within these encounters. There is only one scene in the story, near the end, when the narrator is finally able to consummate a relationship sexually. Again, however, though the scene obviously concludes in sex, the act itself is never described, but only insinuated.

When he learns that his mother is ill, the narrator finally goes to see her in Israel. After visiting his family, he immediately goes to visit Jakub. Instead of Jakub, a woman, Lea, who he assumes is Jakub's maid, opens the door. He describes her as "a dwarfish woman with a monstrously ugly face, and a large head with curls that a hairdresser had arranged" (60). He soon discovers that Lea is actually Jakub's wife, and he again uses two different Polish words, "*monstrum*" and "*potwór*" (monster), to describe her hideousness. The narrator's description of Lea is openly misogynistic, reducing her to an inhuman creature.[12] His assumption is that Jakub married her only to hide from his own homoerotic desires, as he himself seemed willing to do with Maryla when he attempted to propose to her. The hostility the narrator exhibits toward Lea once again reveals Stryjkowski's own revulsion toward female sexuality as evidenced in the earlier *In the Willows*.

His meeting with Jakub becomes heated, as they return to their "dualistic" friendship straddling love and rivalry. In the end, however, the narrator tells Jakub, "You were more than a friend to me," to which Jakub replies, "You for me as well" (68). After leaving Jakub's, he describes a feeling of nausea, as though he had "overcome fear, freed from a great weight." (70). The act of finally admitting his desires to the person who had for so long embodied those desires is an existentially cathartic moment for the narrator. While still in this state, he is approached by an Englishman named John, who first offers to help him find his way around town and then invites him for a drink. After the invitation, the narrator suddenly asks: "'How did you know?' 'It doesn't take a lot for us. The heart begins to beat strongly, so strong it feels like it might burst. Do you not also get such signals? It's the same with desire and fear'" (72). What John describes is akin to what in contemporary parlance would be called "gaydar." The narrator's unfamiliarity with it makes his inexperience with other gay men more obvious. He asks if it is a feeling, "Like just before a crime?" to which John replies, "Like just before sin" (72). The narrator then describes the act as "a bed of husbands," and goes on to say, "For thousands of years my ancestors punished it by stoning. [. . .] Obviously something to fear" (72). This reference to the biblical punishment of stoning for same-sex relationships speaks directly to much of the fear Stryjkowski's narrator feels as a gay man. The threat of death as a result of one's desires is no small matter. However, following his "defeat of fear" after his confrontation with Jakub, the narrator refuses to run as he had earlier. Instead, he leaves with John, and after a long, coded conversation about their desires, John leads the narrator to a hotel: "John took my hand and led me to a room with two beds. 'I'll help you undress.' 'No! No!' I cried, while at the same time stripping off my clothes" (81). Freed from Jakub, far from his Polish homeland, the narrator is finally able to fulfill his desires for another man. Interestingly, the scene ends in an ellipsis, and on the page the text is broken by a noticeably large space. It is in the silence of the ellipsis that the sexual act occurs, but is never described, and remains something that cannot be said. Even though the narrator is finally able to act on his desires, Stryjkowski remains unable to completely describe the fulfillment of them.

I agree with Borkowska's suggestion that ambiguity is "Stryjkowski's narrative strategy," his stories refusing "to explain anything. [. . .] Conflicts remain unresolved and questions remain unanswered" (2002, 55). This ambiguous style—quite similar to Iwaszkiewicz's—in which Stryjkowski approaches the discussion of his sexuality adds a dimension to the title, *Milczenie*. As others have also done, I have translated it as *Silence*. It seems like an obvious title for the book, pointing to the silence to which gay people are forced to adhere, especially in the context of Poland. However, a more common noun in Polish for silence is *"cisza,"* which has the sense of general quiet. The word *"milczenie,"* on the other hand, is a verbal noun created from the infinitive *"milczeć,"* which means to remain quiet, or "to keep from speaking." Indeed, the imperative form, *"milcz,"* is a strong way of telling someone to "shut up." As Stryjkowski himself stated, this was to be his coming-out book, the book through which he would "tear off the veil" from his sexuality. However, throughout the first half of the book he approaches this theme haltingly, only speaking of it in code, and when, finally, there can be no question about his desires, he cannot bring himself to completely describe the sexual act. Leszek Bugajski says of *Silence* that it

> is not a description of joyful self-discovery, or the stabilization of one's identity. Everything is marked by suffering, uncertainty, fear of society's reaction, or the reaction of the object of affection. At the time of the emancipation of homosexuality [. . .] Stryjkowski's stories astound one by what can most easily be called shyness, or even embarrassment. (1993, 114)

Not only has society forced him to remain quiet about his sexuality, but to a certain degree he has also silenced himself.

CONCLUSION

In Stryjkowski's short story "Ajeleth," from his collection *Proper Name*, the main character asks Adam "Where is your homeland?" to which he replies, "My language is my homeland" (1961, 61). Though apparently in harmony with linguistic nationalism, this assertion that language is a homeland actually resists nationalistic views of a homogenous, unitary national identity. Language is at the core of nationalism's expression and maintenance of perceived national coherence. As Stephen Barbour and Cathie Carmichael state in their book *Language and Nationalism in Europe*,

> While the linguistically homogeneous state is extremely rare, and while a high proportion of languages are actually not sharply distinct from others, the demand for the linguistically homogeneous nation and the clearly distinct national language has become a standard part of nationalist ideology. (2000, 14)

Nationalists require a single national language in order to maintain the myth of the unified state. However, not only are there many languages within any national border, but the alleged "national" language itself is always multiple, being divided by accents and dialects. There only ever exists a "perceived monolingualism" (14–15). In expressing his homeland as his language, the multilingual narrator of "Ajeleth" disrupts this nationalist ideal of a monolingual state.

Language is much more fluid than nationalist ideologies would admit. Whereas legal "nationality" might stop at a border, a language does not abide by any such restrictions. Polish does not simply end at Poland's borders where other languages begin, nor do other languages simply stop at their nations' borders and Polish begin. Languages always "cross-pollinate," mix, and influence one another, a fluidity most apparent in border regions where languages meet and blend. Stryjkowski himself was quite familiar with such fluidity, being born and raised in the eastern Kresy of Poland, a historically unstable space marked by an ever shifting cultural landscape. Laura Quercioli Mincer calls it "a world whose rhythms and language are still often archaic and different; a world which [spoke] Yiddish, Ukrainian, and Polish, which [wrote] in German and which [prayed] in Hebrew" (2001, 491). In her book *A Biography of No Place*, Kate Brown calls the area at the time of Stryjkowski's youth a "mosaic of cultures," with "ambiguous and marginal characteristics" (2004, 2). She goes on to describe it as having had an "amorphous, hybrid flexibility," and a "hard-to-pin-down" quality (2, 12). Her description is analogous to Bhabha's notion of the "Third Space," which disrupts "our sense of the historical identity of culture as a homogenizing, unifying force" (1994, 54). And for Antony Polonsky and Monika Adamczyk-Garbowska, Stryjkowski did not have a homeland in "the physical sense; and since for him language is the true mark of identity, he is destined to remain split between his troubled sense of Polishness and the consciousness of his Jewish roots" (2001, xv).

This discussion of language in reference to Stryjkowski's fiction illustrates once again his life-long resistance to limitations on his identity. Stryjkowski spoke and wrote in several languages, meaning that if one's homeland is language, his homeland was multivalent. Adamczyk-Garbowska calls Stryjkowski's situation "trilingual," one in which he combined "disregard and resentment for Yiddish, unfulfilled juvenile love for Hebrew, and a successful long-term romance with Polish." (1998, 381). In a later interview, Stryjkowski returned to this idea of a fluid homeland, saying, "The world is the homeland of the writer." (qtd. in Mincer 2001, 489). This rejection of the static, unitary homeland is a product of Stryjkowski's upbringing in the liminal, interstitial space of the Polish Kresy. This hybrid cultural geography had a clear influence on his work. His narrators see their positions as "strangers everywhere" as points of strength. When they look at the night sky to find

Sirius in "foreign" lands—"foreign" *sous rature* since, as citizens of the world they are never not home—they are not lost. They refuse the requests of one of their communities to deny their other communities.

In *Saved in the East* he told Piotr Szewc that he felt several conflicts within himself (Szewc 1991). He was a Polish Jewish writer who first became a Zionist then a communist. He refused to say kaddish at his own father's funeral, but would later become one of the most prolific memorializers of Judaic Poland. When he wanted to free himself "from the closed world of Judaism, he cut off his side locks and threw away his yarmulke—[yet] he began wearing it again from time to time" in his eighties (Bikont and Szczęsna 2006). The conflict he felt is the cornerstone of his writing. *In the Willows* and *Silence* reveal his rejection of what he saw as the false choice between being Polish and being Jewish, refusing to see them as mutually exclusive identities. In each, Stryjkowski's struggle with this Polish/Jewish binary is made more complicated by his communism and his queer sexuality. Though this tension between his Polishness and Jewishness is not a central theme in *Tommaso del Cavaliere*, the novella does illustrate his wish for homoerotic desire to be part of the public consciousness. That even in his "coming-out" work he felt he could discuss his desires only tangentially says much about the position of queer voices in Poland, even at the end of the twentieth century.

NOTES

1. A shorter version of this chapter was published as an article as "Julian Stryjkowski: Polish, Jewish, Queer," *Canadian Slavonic Papers* 61, no. 1 (2019): pp. 57–80.

2. To date, very little of Stryjkowski's work has been translated into English. These few pieces include *The Inn*, translated by Celina Wieniewska (1972a), and Christopher Garbowski's translations of "Judas Maccabeus: Afterword," (2001a) and excerpts from "Voices in the Darkness" (2001b).

3. Though written in 1946, *Voices in the Dark* was not published until 1956.

4. Similarly to some, I have decided to refer to *In the Willows* as a novel, although others prefer to see it as a collection of short stories. I believe that its designation as a novel is more appropriate. The three chapters, while certainly able to be read as self-contained narratives, together tell a single story. This is most apparent in the appearance of the copper cross in the narrator's dream from the beginning of the novel in "The Swell" and its reappearance around a student's neck at the end of the book in "In the Willows." In both instances the cross is a symbol of the pressure Polish Jews often felt to convert, and it bookends the single volume.

5. I would like to express my gratitude to the International Writing Program at the University of Iowa for allowing me access to Stryjkowski's file in their archives.

6. See McDonough (2011).

7. See Czabanowska-Wróbel (1995, 164).

8. For more on the anti-Jewish campaign of 1967–1968, see Stola (2000).

9. I would like to thank Professor Valeria Sobol for drawing my attention to this reading.

10. I would like to thank Professor Michael Finke for suggesting the connection between "Rothschild's Fiddle" and "In the Willows."

11. Vladimir Zhabotinskii (October '88, 1880—August 4, 1940) was the founder of the Jewish Self-Defence Organization in Odessa.

12. I feel an important intervention that could be made here would be a feminist analysis of the misogyny of this scene. Unfortunately, I feel that it does not entirely fit with the goals of my project as it stands.

Chapter Three

Marian Pankowski

The Anti-Martyr

Thus far I have presented two somewhat distinct approaches to the transgressive project of subverting Polish heteronormativity. The works of Witold Gombrowicz and Jarosław Iwaszkiewicz rely on an emphatic antagonism toward the violence such ideologies employ, while Julian Styrjkowski's very personal work illustrates his desire to reconcile disparate identities—an ultimately subversive act in its privileging of heterogeneity over homogeneity. Though all three authors clearly wish to undermine normative institutions such as nationalism and homophobia, when compared to the work of Marian Pankowski, their approaches seem quite timid. In this chapter I will argue that Pankowski's most well-known work, the novel *Rudolf* (1980 [1984]) constitutes a radical political project in its struggle against the nationalism and martyrology Pankowski saw as deeply imbedded in, and ultimately ruinous of Polish culture. His condemnations of these systems are made through the use of explicit and unabashed queer erotics that subvert all traditional Polish values. I will first briefly discuss two other works that bookend Pankowski's life and career; his 1959 novella *Matuga idzie: przygody* (Here Comes Matuga: Adventures) and his 2000 short memoir *Z Auszwicu Do Belsen: Przygody* (From Auschwitz to Belsen: Adventures), which was short listed for the Nike Literary Award, one of the most prestigious literary prizes in Poland. Though both of these works add to his anti-nationalist and anti-martyrological project, I have decided to focus more on *Rudolf* as it represents a fuller development of it. What is more, because of its use of subversive queer erotics to achieve this goal, the novella more fully fits into the objective of my study as a political intervention.

At a conference of writers held in Poznań in 1992 entitled "Days of Polish Émigré Drama," Pankowski gave a short talk on his status as a Polish émigré author. The title of the talk was "*Garb*" (The Hunchback)—quoted here from its printed version in the journal *Dialog*. According to Pankowski, Polish émigré society was a hunchback, and "though gilded in prayers and poetry, remained a hunchback" (161). It was a culture weighed down by nationalist sentimentalism, by its attempts to maintain the Polish nation and to keep alive the Polish myth of tragedy and exile begun in the eighteenth century at a time when Poland did not even exist as a political reality. Its writers wrote "about far-away Poland as about a cemetery" (162), as a murdered, victimized space. He discusses his decision to eventually leave behind his "émigré identity" as he could no longer abide the messianic ideology of Polish Romanticism that continued to influence Polish cultural thought throughout the post-communist period. This decision was inspired by his studies with Claude Backvis, a Belgian Slavist who was lecturing on Polish literature. Pankowski says, "he approached our Romanticism with admiration, but without solemnity. With polite irony he ignored messianism, and above all else praised the creativity" of the Polish Romantics (162). This approach to the study of Polish Romantic poetry was for Pankowski something utterly novel. Instead of the reader being struck dumb in awe of the almost mythical poets, their "artistry and craftsmanship [. . .] became recognized as the main criterion" (162). Pankowski's rejection of Romantic messianism and his pointed criticisms of Polish culture became the central themes of much of his work.

Pankowski was born in 1919 in Sanok, in what is today southeastern Poland. In 1938 he began his authorial career with the publication of a few poems, and in the same year began his studies at the Jagiellonian University in Kraków. These studies were cut short by the Nazi invasion of Poland the following year. He would soon after join the army, and later fight with the Polish Resistance, only to be arrested in 1942 by the Gestapo "on charges of belonging to the underground army Union of Armed Struggle" (De Bruyn et al., 2011, 468), which eventually became the Home Army (Armia Krajowa, AK). He would spend the rest of the war in several concentration camps—Auschwitz, Gross-Rosen, Nordhausen, and Bergen-Belsen. The numbers "46 333," the tattoo he received on his forearm after becoming an inmate, appear regularly in his works. After being freed from the camps, he moved to Brussels, where he found "an island of joy. Clad and fed by allied philanthropic institutions, he lived in an illusion of normality [. . .] a miniature society, whose exilic myth was its constitution" (Pankowski 1993, 161). He would from that point on be known as an "émigré" author, a moniker he was never comfortable with, preferring to be known as a "Pole living abroad" (De Bruyn et al., 2011, 470), illustrating a distaste for the exilic mythos. He finally finished his PhD in Slavic Studies, writing his dissertation on Bolesław Leśmian at the Free University in Brussels in 1963. He then became a Professor of Slavic at the same university, where he continued to work until the 1980s. He remained in Brussels until his death in April 2011.

Early on in his life abroad Pankowski began writing and publishing fiction. His most important work, *Rudolf*, published in 1980 and released in Poland in 1984, "created a scandal, and numerous critics accused Pankowski of pornography and immorality" (Adamowski 2011). Renata Gorczyńska called it a "manifesto of sexual anarchy" (1988, 161). These criticisms, and Pankowski's incessant satirizing of Polish culture, would keep him from gaining wider notoriety in Poland until only quite recently. He spoke and wrote in French fluently, but never wrote in French first, though he knew the original Polish versions of his prose had very little chance of being read in Poland. He refused to give up publishing in his first language. This was even at a time when French and Dutch translations of his fiction and stagings of his dramatic work were becoming quite popular in Francophone Western Europe and the Low Countries (De Bruyn et al., 2011, 471). Writing and publishing first in French would almost have guaranteed him a much wider audience, especially in the Anglophone world—*Rudolf* remains his only work ever translated into English.[1] It has only been quite recently that extensive study of Pankowski's work has begun.

Pankowski's choice of language is another possible reason that only one of his novels has been translated into English, and that very little scholarship about him exists in English. In her essay "Marian Pankowski's Fury of Words," Renata Gorczyńska discusses Pankowski's heavy use of village dialect, local neologisms, and mixing in of foreign words. This style makes the translation of his texts extremely difficult. One is constantly trying to find words in translation dictionaries that do not even exist in Polish dictionaries. Gorczyńska goes so far as to claim that Pankowski is more interested in *"how* to say something rather than *what* to say" (1988, 159). However, it seems to me that Pankowski is actually engaged in a postmodern move to erase the lines between form and content. While it is true that the language he uses is extremely experimental, the subject matter of his works is just as important. The subject matter is so extreme that the form of expression one must use to discuss it also takes on a radical character. In his essay "The Darknesses of Marian Pankowski," Ryszard K. Przybylski sees something similar in Pankowski's style. For Przybylski it is as if Pankowski had said, "I will connect what, in your opinion cannot be connected. I will mix oppositions. Everything will lose its distinctions: heaven and earth, soul and body. And also languages: hieratic or plebian, literary or low jargon" (1993, 163). As I will note in my analysis of *Rudolf,* Pankowski's style relied on the mixing of the high and low, the vulgar and the sublime. This again is a postmodern move, bringing the popular into the realm of the literary.

MATUGA AND AUSCHWITZ

Here Comes Matuga was only Pankowski's second published work of prose after *Tanned Freedom* (1955), a small collection of short stories. Before these he had mainly written poetry and drama. With his break from writing poetry it became clear that Pankowski wished to devote his writing toward pointing a critical finger at the "various Polish complexes, [and] anachronisms" he found in Polish society (Adamowski 2011). Pankowski even once called *Matuga* a "text of rebellion [. . .] the manifesto of a poet pounding against the voice of the national literature" (1993, 162). With his prose Pankowski wished to engage in a very clear critical project against outdated modes of national identity creation. Jolanta Pasterska views Pankowski's prose as "a polemic against the national tradition and history, which are so strongly rooted in Romanticism" (2011, 527). *Matuga* is made up of loosely bound stories centered on the character Władziu Matuga, an emigrant from a country the narrator names "Potatoland" (Kartoflania). Krystyna Ruta-Rutkowska sees in *Matuga* "a sarcastic destruction of codes of the great national literature; [in particular] the code of *Pan Tadeusz*" (2008, 35), the Romantic epic by Adam Mickiewicz. The work begins parodying "Pan Tadeusz" on the very opening page. The first "chapter" is a kind of invocation entitled "To the Reader." It includes the line: "And all is girdled as though with a grassy ribbon . . . Not girdled. Cut through with a razor, straight and to the bone" (1983, 12). The first part of this line is a direct quotation of line 21 from "Pan Tadeusz" in Mickiewicz's description of the Lithuanian countryside. The narrator of *Matuga*, however, does not see the idyll Mickiewicz imagined. Instead, he bears witness to the destroyed landscape of post-war Poland, "cut through with a razor." Like Mickiewicz, who wrote while in exile in France and Dresden, the narrator of *Matuga* is also writing outside the nation. However, unlike Mickiewicz, the narrator's experiences, which include internment in concentration camps—mirroring Pankowski's own life—will not allow him to romanticize the Polish situation. It is an audacious act on the part of Pankowski to set himself up against the bard of Polish literature. Ruta-Rutkowska sees this "anti-Mickiewiczian" move further illustrated in the heroes of each work. Whereas Matuga is continually moving on—"idzie," "going"—Tadeusz returns home to stay. "Thus he reverses the model of the static, neighbourly and social existence, inscribed in Mickiewicz's work. The provincial, naïve Pole has been replaced by a hero who has decided to have an adventure with the world" (2008, 542). The parodying of the Polish mythos continues in the following chapter entitled "Potatoland." This will be the moniker the narrator uses to refer to Poland throughout the rest of the work. In renaming Poland with this satirical title, Pankowski is criticizing the provincialism and small-mindedness he believed to be endemic to Polish culture. He makes an interesting word choice in Polish when he uses "*Karto-*

flania," from "kartofel," instead of creating a word from the more Polish "*ziemniak*." "*Kartofel*" is a borrowing from German, and though certainly understood in Polish, it is used more often in the countryside. The chapter tells of the wonders of the potato for Matuga's country, of its "eternal potato-tude" (12). The coming of the potato to the land is described in an old book entitled

> On the Miraculous Bestowing of the Potato to Our Country: Or On the Undying Care of Heaven and Above all of Our Advocate, Written According to the Voices Coming from High by Justyna Of the Hunger, in the Office of the Franciscan Patala, In the Year of Our Lord Suchandsuch. (13)

The rest of the chapter describes this "miraculous bestowing" of the potato, parodying the style of hagiography. It also uses a more classic Polish vocabulary and grammar, such as the ending "ey" instead of "ej" for the feminine genitive. Not only is Pankowski satirizing Polish provincialism, but also religiosity and superstition. The rest of the novella continues unrelentingly in this satirical mode.

In *From Auschwitz to Belsen* Pankowski takes on the slightly different project of refuting the mythology of Polish suffering during the Second World War, especially as reflected in art about surviving the camps. Bożena Shallcross notes that "Polish concentration camp literature [is] dominated by a martyrological model" (2011, 513), a model to which Pankowski refused to adhere. While under communist control, rhetoric about the Holocaust in Poland was that Poles, and not Jews, were the primary victims of the Nazis. This would remain the official and only legal Communist Party line until the Round Table agreement of 1989. Of course, this reading of history was rarely challenged within Poland during the People's Republic (PRL), and even remains a not-uncommon view among Poles today. This was clearly illustrated by the Auschwitz Cross disputes of 1998 and 1999 when hundreds of small crosses were erected just outside the concentration camp in protest of plans to remove a cross that had been placed there during a mass by Pope John Paul II.[2] The heroism of the martyr has played a central role in Polish culture since the Romantics' invention of the messianic notion of Poland as the "Christ of Nations" in the nineteenth century. In *From Auschwitz*, Pankowski constantly undermines this heroic narrative, going so far as to question the extent of his own suffering in the camps. He is approached by a group asking survivors of the camps to fill out questionnaires. At one point he says to himself, "the capos rarely beat us. It was dry and warm in the metal-works. And so what? After all I can't tell that to Professor X., the author of the aforementioned questionnaire" (2000, 15). Though his imprisonment was certainly horrific, and he was even tortured at one point, he admits that what he experienced was not equivalent to the fate of Jewish victims. Piotr Krupiński makes the excellent point of the importance in distinguishing the difference between the "concentration camp" and the "extermination camp" in his essay on Pankowksi's anti-martyrological literature (2011, 555). Yet the researchers and documentarians who create these questionnaires are invested in the same mythos of Polish suffering. He is asked, "there... in Auschwitz... you didn't feel unhappy?" He replies, "Maybe I did feel this, and maybe I really was unhappy, but I didn't know it. Probably because I had freed myself of my own time" (24). He avoids using his own suffering as a kind of moral capital, treating his imprisonment as insignificant in comparison to the experiences of others. He calls his camp experiences a "retreat," when compared to the "Warsaw boys who, bare handed, turned over German tanks like turning over turtles" (35). Despite the suffering he experienced, he feels guilty for having been in the "safety" of a concentration camp while the Warsaw Uprising was taking place.

RUDOLF

The satire against nationalism in *Matuga,* and the anti-martyrological project in *From Auschwitz* coalesce in his most well-known work, *Rudolf.* Though rather short, consisting of only 110 pages, *Rudolf* is extremely dense in language and theme. The narrative relates the interactions between a Polish-born professor of Slavic at a Belgian university—which mirrors Pankowski's own biography, bringing to mind the autofictitious—and a gay, German-Polish pensioner, the titular Rudolf. The narrative mainly focuses on their relationship, whether in face-to-face conversation or through the letters they write one another. The story begins with a kind of dividing and doubling, similar to what takes place in Gombrowicz's *TransAtlantyk* when Gombrowicz-the-character first comes across Gonzalo.[3] The narrator, whose name we never learn, begins a conversation with a retired gentleman sitting alone in the Grand Place of Brussels. He experiences a kind of recognition in this older man. Like the narrator, the Polish-born professor living abroad in Belgium, the older gentleman is also a stranger. Eventually we discover that he is an ethnic German, born in Poland, now also living abroad in Belgium. When he first approaches Rudolf the narrator tells him in French, "I live here, I belong here" (1996, 9).[4] Despite a claim to belonging to Belgium, the narrator understands that this belonging is complicated by his own biography as an ethnic Pole. The narrator and Rudolf are doubles because of their mutual "un-belonging." This becomes more apparent as they continue speaking. Though they had been conversing in French, Rudolf is able to see that the narrator is Polish, asking him, "You're a Pole?" (11). This flusters the narrator and he responds, "I don't see what that's got to do with . . . yes, a Pole . . . when we're here having a chat in French . . . besides, I've been here for thirty years . . . so that . . . you know . . . we . . . Europeans" (11). The narrator is not quite denying his Polishness, but he is making a choice to identify as a European instead. Soon after this Rudolf lets slip a "ja-ja!" The narrator realizes that he is German, thinking to himself, "he's reddened, because that '*ja-ja*' of his has betrayed a Germanic shirt. Let's take our chance, since our boxer has lowered his guard: 'You're . . . German?'" (11). This hiding and revealing of national backgrounds takes on an antagonistic character. By calling Rudolf a "boxer" the narrator reveals the conversation to be a kind of struggle between the two. It is a strange reversal of nationalistic disputes in which the antagonists' vocal admissions and declarations of their national identities are central to the argument. Here, instead, the two attempt to keep their national identities hidden for as long as possible, preferring the more cosmopolitan "European" moniker. Just like the narrator, when Rudolf's Germanness is revealed he also refuses it, instead saying, "Yes . . . but from now on . . . we're going to speak Polish!" (11). They will use Polish throughout the rest of the text in both their conversations and the letters they exchange. Rudolf then relates his life story, beginning with his birth in Łódź, Poland. Rudolf's biography, that of an ethnic German born and raised in Poland, demands the reader acknowledge the contentious history of post–Second World War Poland behind that biography. It creates a problematic ethnic and national identity for Rudolf, who appears to be one of millions of Germans forced to leave Poland after the end of the war. The contentiousness of the encounter is stressed further when the narrator likens their conversation to their being soldiers: "as we run we've crossed Europe, and by now each of us is seated in his own dugout, waiting. With a bayonet" (12). Again, however, the nature of their battle is a satirical reversal of the nationally and racially charged reasons Europe had gone to war previously. Now, instead of nations warring with one another over national superiority, two representatives of nations are warring over who can hide their national identity better. What is most revealing in the exchange is Rudolf's insistence that they speak Polish. His attempt at a position of superiority is actually strengthened by subordinating his primary, "ethnic" language. It is in the third space of Belgium, neither Poland nor Germany, where this kind of soft war can occur, and the obstacles of their shared history can fall away.

Another doubling takes place during their conversation as the scene in the Place is intermingled with an erotic scene of two young men driving through the Belgian countryside. It describes the two men finding a stream where they wash each other, being observed the entire time by a young goatherd, who eventually becomes so excited that he must urinate. The movements between the two scenes are sudden, with no obvious link between them. They are separated by setting and characters, yet Pankowski wishes them to be brought together. The erotic idyll in the one scene opposes the aged banality of the other. Eroticism, and more importantly, queer eroticism becomes an important element of the story from the very beginning. The two scenes, though narratively and thematically unconnected, come to be structurally interlinked. This connectedness demands we read something of the youth and eroticism of the one scene in the other. It is a suggestion of some remaining youthful vitality still left in the two older men, a suggestion that despite their age they continue to be sexual beings. The mix of these two elements—the anti-national character of the conversation between the narrator and Rudolf, and the homoeroticism of the scene between the two young men—becomes the leitmotif of the novella. It is setting the Eros of queer desire against the Thanatos of nationalism and normativity.

Early into their conversation, Rudolf reveals his sexual identity to the narrator, saying, "Ever since my school days only one thing's mattered: boys" (14). This unabashed declaration shocks the narrator and his reaction proves to be a model for his future reactions to the descriptions of Rudolf's erotic life. The narrator attempts to make logical, normative sense of Rudolf's queer desires. His first response is to say, "well . . . tastes differ [. . .] these things happen . . . and viewing the matter statistically" (14). It is impossible for the narrator to understand one man's desire for another, yet ultimately his responses illustrate a denial of the importance of pleasure of any kind. He ends by telling Rudolf, "I feel quite simply that I'm a member of society in the full sense . . . in teaching . . . I try to keep faith with certain principles which for centuries . . . have been handed down from generation to generation" (15). This statement draws an immediate, visceral reaction from Rudolf, the narrator describing him as "leaping up" (15):

> My good sir! What's this that's "been handed down from generation to generation?" "Thou shalt love they neighbor as thyself" no doubt? Society?! Rogues and sycophants always to the fore! And knowledge—good for riffling through rancid encyclopedias [. . .] to add new molds to old! [. . .] But my good sir, what's that got to do with a man of flesh and blood, with you, with me?! [. . .] Do you know what counts? Joy . . . pleasure . . . to . . . dilate in a flash, as if a good half-dozen lungs inside you are starting to breathe frosty air. (15–16)

Here Rudolf articulates his philosophy of *jouissance*, calling for "joy" and "pleasure" as opposed to received notions of "acceptable" morality. He begins by trivializing classically privileged values of Western culture such as tradition, society, knowledge, and Christian pieties, calling them "petty," and reducing them to little more than "new molds" that can be added to older ones. For Rudolf, these values accomplish little, and he views them as only serving their own self-reproduction. He reverses the paradigm, valuing the corporeal, the human, the base, but also the present and fleeting as opposed to quasi "eternal" generations. Instead of privileging the ability to recite "the uses of the genitive singular"—the mind, the logical—he wants society to value the "frosty air" inside our lungs—the body, the sensual. It is a defense of joy and life against a self-destructive culture of death.

Immediately following Rudolf's "call to joy," the narrative moves into a flashback scene, related in a stream of consciousness. It is not conveyed by the narrator, but instead it is meant to be understood as a look directly into Rudolf's memories. The scene depicts what will be called the "forbidden ball." It describes a group of high-class gentlemen, Rudolf being among them, arriving at a manor house in winter after a day of hunting. They begin drinking, and then dancing with the farmhands. Eventually the group breaks off into pairs, each gentleman going off with one of the workers. The class divisions of the group are underlined by the descriptions of "peasant trousers thrown down anyhow" and "the metropolitan *plus fours* right next to the trousers" (18). Once again, as seen in *Ferdydurke, The Teacher,* and *Trans-Atlantyk*,[5] the country manor seems to be a space where sexual transgression is, perhaps not fully legitimized, but at least where it is accepted as part of masculine life. It must be reiterated, however, that within these special loci of queer sex, one element common to them all is the presence of a hierarchical class system. The farmhand is never in a position equal to that of his sexual partner, illustrating that a transgression is not necessarily a productive act in dismantling normative regimes.

The text then moves out of the stream-of-consciousness mode. Reflecting on the forbidden ball, Rudolf says, "Ah, my dear man . . . that stink of sweat on a body you don't know, muscles [. . .] without ladies' lard, so that it's all tendons and just like a lumber yard, hacking and hewing away" (19). It is an unashamed, unapologetic articulation of Rudolf's desires. In the context of Polish literature, Rudolf's refusal to be ashamed and his celebration of the male body constitute a political act. He sets himself against the "society" that the narrator wishes to defend. This is stressed further when Rudolf describes how "Olek squirted over those family photographs, the horse boy, over those white ladies at watering places, over those children with little baskets for scattering flowers beneath the priest's feet, over those landowners with curved sabers—so it ran down the walls" (19). The description of his lover climaxing over these images is Rudolf's repudiation of not only heteronormativity but normativity of any kind. It is a debasement of family, society, religion, and—with the mention of "landowners with curved sabers"—traditional *szlachta* Polish life. He has undermined the social structures these images represent through Olek's defilement. Later, reflecting deeper on his relationship with Olek, Rudolf reveals to the narrator that he had first met him in a public restroom, and that they had first had sex in a park, "on the fresh green grass!" (28). It is a reminder of the danger gay people have endured, and in many places continue to endure, in order to achieve even a modicum of intimacy. It is not always a "forbidden ball" in a country manor where local farmhands can be bought for two zloties; it is more often than not an endeavor fraught with the repercussions of social, and sometimes legal restriction.

Despite the seeming vulgarity of the descriptions of his encounters with Olek, Rudolf ends his story by saying, "We loved each other for twelve years, Olek and I" (31). The narrator, as a representative of normative hegemony, can only understand Rudolf's story about Olek if it fits into some kind of mythical order. When Rudolf asks if his relationship with Olek strikes the narrator as funny, he replies no, "Every way of keeping faith . . . or even . . . well . . . . In this earthly chaos of ours order deserves esteem" (31). Rudolf only laughs at this and replies, "Get away with your 'keeping faith' . . . We suited each other. That's all . . . my dear man, that's a lot!" (31). Rudolf sees no need in making his relationships with men "mean" something more. The narrator, to the contrary, is driven to viewing this transgressive behavior as somehow "keeping faith" with some kind of universal order. For Rudolf his love of Olek is enough. This poignant expression of love following such explicit portrayals of sex is the most jarring element of Rudolf's story. Love is not limited to the realm of heteronormative Romantic poetry. It is also expressed through the body and through sex, an act that involves "squirtings," "arses," "muscles," and "hewing away." For Rudolf love is physical, and involves the beautiful messiness of the human body. Rudolf's mingling of "poignant" love and the "vulgar" elements of lovemaking emphasizes the humanity of his affair with Olek, once again reiterating his privileging of joy and pleasure. In raising the base and vulgar Rudolf is attempting to rob regimes of normativity of some of their power to regulate bodies and acts of love. He will not be regulated. His use of vulgar, explicit language in depictions of sex is a form of reterritorialization, overthrowing heteronormative systems of morality and replacing them with his own morality of jouissance.

Rudolf's resistance to regulation is illustrated further when he and the narrator begin discussing the war. When asked how he spent the war, Rudolf says he continued "hunting," meaning having trysts with young men and soldiers, and avoided having to serve in the military until almost the very end. "And when the Germans came looking for partisans, I'd say: 'Partisans? Here?' They'd take a German at his word" (21). Rudolf's disinterested attitude toward serving the German nation in a time of war shocks the narrator, who again was expecting some kind of expression of nationalist sentiment. "Everything's topsy-turvy in my mind. I was just thinking I'd pin this vast black, yellow, and red butterfly down, and now the colors have scattered off its wings. Any minute . . . the next thing will be . . . it's he who's the patriot!" (21–22). Unlike Rudolf, the narrator is still invested in the battle between them to prove who is the more cosmopolitan, the more European. The narrator continues to define Rudolf only by his Germanness, as represented by the "black, yellow, and red" colors of the post–Second World War German flag. Rudolf, however, refuses "to be pinned down" by any mode of national identification. His refusal to fight for the fatherland, and his impulse to work against it, threatens the narrator's own self-definition as a defender of Polish culture and society. In an attempt to gain some kind of moral high ground over Rudolf, the narrator slowly rolls up his sleeve to reveal the tattoo on his forearm, the numbers "46 333," which he received in Auschwitz. It is a martyrological act, an attempt to use his suffering to validate and increase his authority.

However, the effect it has on Rudolf is unexpected. Instead of admitting the currency of the narrator's suffering, he quips: "My dear man . . . what's to be said to THAT? It's a kind of holy image . . . you don't know whether to wipe it away or put it in a little frame and stop living and do nothing but light a candle in front of it. . . . That's why I've never liked looking at cripples" (22). On the one hand Rudolf acknowledges the "sanctity" of the suffering the tattoo represents—it should be treated as a holy icon. And yet, though it should be the ultimate symbol of suffering, Rudolf considers it mundane and insignificant, repudiating its martyrological value in much the same way Pankowski does in *From Auschwitz*. Despite Rudolf's reaction, the narrator refuses to back down and presses the point: "I thrust this number right under his gaze. And he sees these corpselike figures advancing on his baggy eyes, sees that I'm driving these gray geese up to his muzzle" (22). In response Rudolf opens his shirt to reveal his own tattoo scrawled across his belly, "of Afro-Asio-design! Tattooed in violet and livid green. Not quite minarets, not quite pricks roused by a spring wind, as so much of it is dancing erection and bamboo parallels" (22). When Rudolf displays his tattoo he is setting the "life" it represents against the "death" the narrator's tattoo represents. Instead of "corpselike figures" tattooed over the veins that might be sliced when a person commits suicide, Rudolf presents "roused pricks," "spring wind," and "dancing" that are tattooed across the belly, the house of carnal pleasures. It is yet another repudiation of the thanatic with the erotic. This repudiation is stressed further when we learn that the tattoo spells the name "Yazit," a young Arab with whom Rudolf had maintained a long relationship years earlier, calling it "love" and not "jailbird filth" (24). Once again Rudolf conflates the vulgar and the sublime. Though Yazit had been a prostitute, he remembers him lovingly, and not as something lower than himself.

As a kind of epilogue to their war of tattoos the narrator mentions seeing several tattooed men in the concentration camps: "One of them had . . . tattooed on his back . . . you know . . . a ginger cat. And this cat was chasing a pearly gray mouse half-hidden . . . guess where!" (23). Rudolf finds the story funny, but then replies: "Sure I can guess where . . . but you see . . . what they've done to you . . . mother, school, and priests! Instead of saying the mouse is running up his arse . . . you wrap it up in euphemisms, in stutterings" (24). He repeats this sentiment later when he tells the narrator that it is "women teachers and priests who've instilled in us Poles that mania for washing our hands and a superstitious fear of breasts at the backs of our bodies, from between which oozes the unending serpent of our uncleanliness, expelled from paradise" (40). For Rudolf the systems that attempt to regulate bodies and desires are not supported by agents who represent a nebulous officialdom. Instead these systems are maintained by the everyday proxies of morality. The fear of "breasts at the backs of our bodies" infers the fear of being a receiver of penetrative anal sex, "the serpent" symbolizing both the serpent of *Genesis* and the erect penis. This is a source of pollution, of "uncleanliness" and "ooze" that leads to punishment and expulsion from proper society. The "mothers" and "priests" have made it impossible for the narrator to even speak directly about the anus, let alone recognize its potential as a site of pleasure. In her analysis of a scene from *Here Comes Matuga*, Bożena Shallcross uses Guy Hocquenghem's work *Homosexual Desire* (1972) to note that the anus, as the source of distinction between normative and non-normative sexualities, "should not be exposed or even alluded to. Since the anus and anal penetration, associated with excrement, are excluded from social life, the very fact of homosexual desire and its satisfaction via the anus implies crossing the boundaries of social normativity" (2011, 515).

For Rudolf, the maintenance of the "boundaries of social normativity" implies stasis and death. He believes that one must transgress the laws of the "mothers and priests" in order to truly live a full life. He recognizes the productive power of transgression, and repeatedly defends it against the arguments of the narrator, who throughout their exchanges remains a stalwart supporter of Culture, viewing transgression as unproductive and wasteful. He continually disparages Rudolf's past actions, as when, in response to his relationship with Olek, he states that Rudolf was just a young man "from a good family" who wanted to "tear his Sunday clothes on a nail, as it were [. . .] you wanted to get free of the civilized world. [. . .] And on this impulse, you transgressed another city limit. . . . But I repeat, you went with the *intention* of trespassing" (33). It remains inconceivable for the narrator that Rudolf might have experienced affection and love in his relationships with other men. According to him, Rudolf's affairs were little more than the actions of a petulant, rebellious teenager. For the narrator, Rudolf's lovemaking with men is bound up with transgressing "limits," or crossing borders. These are social limits, created and maintained by society's "mothers and priests." Again, he is unable to speak of non-normative sexual acts except through the euphemisms of "tearing clothes on a nail," or "transgressing limits." Ultimately the narrator sees these "transgressions" as breaking laws in that they end in "trespassing," which implies a more serious element of illegality.[6] Rudolf's actions are not merely the breaking of social norms; they are dangerous, juridical offenses that must be controlled.

In a letter to Rudolf, the narrator describes seeing hustlers at work in the streets of Paris, and witnessing one going off with a customer. He then writes that one of the other prostitutes winked at him "significantly," which immediately made him run off, because "one cannot run the risk of ridicule after all" (38). In his reply, Rudolf writes:

> And if you had gone with the one who winked so "significantly," maybe you would have forgotten, if only for an hour, your. [. . .] foibles. [. . .] and later maybe he would have begun to talk. And out from under that creature who was playing clever buggers on the street corner would have crawled a human being . . . no doubt lonely . . . like you . . . only less ingenious. Precision is blinding you. [. . .] And that is why you checked over the ones near the drugstore not as brothers in loneliness but as renegades from the ordinary world, to which you are proud to assign yourself. [. . .] Because to fraternize means leaving your patent-leather shoes in the church porch and going barefoot, into the unknown . . . and that is not for you. (38)

Rudolf sees this as a missed opportunity for the narrator, a moment when he could have realized the freedom of transgression, to have finally gotten to know the humanity of the hustler and to realize that it is the same humanity as his own. However, as Rudolf understands, the narrator remains too invested in the "ordinary world," in the systems of normativity that regulate and maintain order. To admit the "renegades," the transgressors into society, is to admit to the artificiality of the borders that society has constructed. For Rudolf this can all be blamed on the narrator's desire for "precision," a desire to be able to clearly define limits, whether national, gender, or any other.

To allow oneself not to be restricted by this precision is to open oneself up to a wider world of joys and pleasures, to "fraternize," and to "go barefoot into the unknown." Pankowski's use of "fraternize," Polish *"bratać się,"* literally "to brother," immediately brings to mind Gombrowicz once again. In his novel *Ferdydurke* the character Miętus wishes to "fra . . . ter . . . nize" with a farmhand. The stuttering of the word speaks to the ineffability of homoerotic interactions between men. In both works "fraternizing," "brothering" is both an act of simple communion between people, as well as a metaphor for gay male sex. The narrator, however, will have none of it. When they meet again later in the story, he tells Rudolf, "you're afraid of law and order . . . of nature's order . . . of health. . . . You prefer a world drooling with secretions . . . festering" (94). For the narrator the only thing that can come from Rudolf's transgressive desires is pollution; however, Rudolf retorts, "like the birch tree, like the body, like the thaw that makes valleys fertile with slime!" (94). This exchange succinctly illustrates the struggle between Rudolf and the narrator. Whereas the narrator sees Rudolf's transgressions as destructive, Rudolf sees them as productive. For the narrator, transgressive desire introduces corruption, but for Rudolf it has an almost life-giving force, a view that stands in opposition to nationalist, heteronormative values that see the homosexual as useless and wasteful, as death. Once again it is an illustration of the opposition between a cult of life—the erotic—and a cult of death—the thanatic. Ironically, they both see transgression as creating the conditions for permeability and fluidity; however, while the narrator believes this to be dangerous, Rudolf believes it to be absolutely necessary for life.

Rudolf's defense of transgression is at its core a defense of bodily joy and pleasure. It becomes an indictment of not just Polish, but of any culture that would restrict such pleasure, and the nationalistic maintenance of rigid bodies central to those cultures. Rudolf's critical stance against nationalism is seen early in the novella in his embarrassment in being "found out" as a German, and in his actions during the war refusing to support the invading German army. His response was to run from a national identity in order not to be "pinned down," as the narrator had attempted. Although he seemingly prefers a Polish identity at the beginning, it becomes apparent that he is critical of all national modes of identification when he directs his criticism toward Polish nationalist ideology. He tells the narrator that Poles

> behave as though every single one of them, without exception, spent his life on horseback. . . . But on horseback, all you can do is give orders, knock off Turks' heads with your saber to add flavor to Viennese coffee, but you can't lower your pants either in front or behind. You can't use your body except for carrying a standard, lance, or holy images. [. . .] You know . . . I believe in riding too. The African continent really thundered under us when I mounted Yazit. . . . But when he'd stretch me at full gallop, spur and goad me on—to the point where Paris began to heal over! Man! Cavalry times! (79)

Rudolf's criticism of Polish nationalism is directly linked to his valorizing of transgressive desires, which are antithetical to normative values that seek to sustain tightly closed systems, such as bodies and nations. His referencing of "sabers," "cavalry times," "knocking off Turks' heads," and "Viennese coffee," all point to the last period of Polish history when Poland was a military power, the seventeenth century. He is specifically referring to the Battle of Vienna in 1683, which was won by the Polish King Jan Sobieski III against the Ottoman Empire after he led a cavalry charge that broke the siege. This event remains an important touchstone of national pride for Poles. In Rudolf's mind their insistence to harken back to this moment from four hundred years earlier is worthy of satire and ridicule. He begins with the very practical concern of one being unable to lower one's pants, "either in front or behind." All the body on horseback can be used for is war. Poles' preoccupation with this mythical heroic past makes it impossible for them to enjoy the pleasures of the body, which is restricted to the job of maintaining the national mythos. He then contrasts this mythos with his own "cavalry" experiences—that is, his sexual exploits with Yazit. This "bare-back" riding is for Rudolf much more important than the Battle of Vienna as it reaffirms his devotion to joy and pleasure. That Yazit was an Arab, that Rudolf had been "fraternizing" with the enemy, strengthens his denial of the power this historic moment is supposed to have for national Polish pride. Reuel K. Wilson sees Pankowski as poking "fun at cliché-ridden Polish nationalism and its passion for myth-making" (1997, 829). I would suggest that what Pankowski accomplishes is more than mere "poking fun," especially in the context of Polish nationalism and mythos. In Polish tradition these themes are vital components of the culture, and in the formation of a national identity. Any satirizing of them constitutes a serious break of the social contract. Rudolf finishes his invective against the Polish cavalry by telling the narrator,

> You're still young . . . try to escape. Try to leap clear of your horse while there's time, run to some alder stream, throw off all your worldly trappings, step into the water. . . . And before you know where you are, some shepherd will be washing your head, shoulders, and back, so that all of a sudden you'll see the meaning of water, birds, light, and brotherhood *with your body*! (80)

Rudolf's advice to the narrator is to leave the "Polish cavalry," the ideology of restriction and traditional values behind. The narrator's best hope is to deny the cult of death fundamental to Polish nationalism, and instead to affirm the cult of life in joy and pleasure. Rudolf rejects the logos, and calls for the narrator to understand the world "bodily," reversing the mind/body binary, privileging the "knowledge" one achieves through "fraternization." In mentioning a shepherd washing the narrator in a stream, the text ties the narrative back to the beginning of the story, referencing the two young men driving through the Belgian countryside and washing each other in a river alongside the road. This asks the reader to return to the earlier scene, folding the story on itself, once again adding an element of the double to the opening pages.

One final scene that further illustrates the novella's satirical take against Polish nationalism occurs while the narrator is visiting Kraków, where he says he feels "a feigned foreignness confronting this town that doesn't remember me" (68). He describes a parade with "lads impersonating scythe-bearing Polish rebels of two hundred years back, who are hurriedly stuffing their jeans in their boot legs so as to turn themselves into those authentic peasant heroes" (69). He notes the "rococo folksiness" of the people in Łowicz skirts (74). These costumes are muddled, taken from various areas of Poland, not uniform, and worn to profess a contrived patriotic feeling. The "scythe-bearing" men are engaged in a reenactment of the Battle of Racławice, in which Tadeusz Kościuszko led a peasant army against the Russian Empire in 1794. The Łowicz folk costume has no place in Kraków, which has its own style of folk dress. What is more, he soon discovers that the parade he is witnessing is to celebrate the re-dedication of the Grunwald

Monument, which took place in 1976, replacing the original 1910 statue that had been destroyed by the occupying Nazis. Not only, then, are the folk costumes muddled, but the history the reenactors are celebrating took place nearly four hundred years later than the Battle of Grunwald. The narrator is describing simulacra upon simulacra: this Grunwald Monument is memorializing an earlier monument that memorialized a battle that took place centuries earlier in a place hundreds of miles from Kraków, in a ceremony attended by "inauthentic" peasants. In her reading of this scene Jolanta Pasterska sees in it "the artificiality of History being brought to life" (2011, 531). These battles are important historical touchstones for Polish nationalist feeling, much like the Battle of Vienna Rudolf references earlier. However, in their insistence on clinging to these heroic legends, the participants are accepting a life of stasis, remaining in a mythical past. This satirical take on the contrived patriotism of ceremony is reflected in a sentiment Pankowski expressed in "The Hunchback" when he called for his countrymen not to be "repeaters of history while singing old songs under famous monuments," but to be instead "dissenters of dogmas" (1993, 162). The scene turns hallucinatory as the statue wrests itself from its platform and begins chasing the narrator through the streets of Kraków. He is captured by the "insurrectionists" bearing scythes and forced into a folk dance. Ironically he calls himself an "anachronistic civilian" (74), since he is the only one not dressed as a peasant or in period costume. His attempt to fit into the act is hindered when his "Parisian Saint-Laurent tie gets hooked on [his] neighbor's scythe" (74). His cosmopolitanism and "Europeanness" will not allow him reentry into Polish culture. Similarly to the satire found in *Matuga*, the scene is critical of the inauthenticity and simplemindedness found in rote expressions of patriotism.

A vital element in expressions of nationalist ideology is the belief that the individual should sacrifice him/herself for the good of the nation. The sanctity of national suffering was central to Polish Romanticism, especially to the messianic notion of Poland as a "Christ of Nations." Some of the most potent assertions of patriotic feeling are the memorializing of national tragedies, and the refusal of the nation to let go of past suffering. Indeed, the remembrance of past national tragedy is often a more effective means of creating patriotic fervor than the remembrance of national victories. It is quite telling that in Poland the largest yearly commemorations for the Second World War are observances of the massacre at Katyń, and the Ghetto and Warsaw Uprisings held at their respective monuments—two imposing monolithic sculptures—though they are essentially commemorating catastrophic defeats at the hands of the Nazis. On an individual level, Krystyna Latawiec notes that in their remembrances of local histories, "people fix their traumas and use them to build the basis of their identity" (2011, 544). Throughout the story Rudolf repeatedly disavows this morality of suffering, as when he counters the narrator's concentration camp tattoo with his own. Rudolf refuses to acknowledge the martyrological authority such suffering is supposed to impart to its victims. This refusal once again reflects a devotion to his personal creed of joy and pleasure, and an opposition to what he sees as nationalist celebrations of suffering. At one point the narrator himself describes this celebration of the martyr in Poland, saying that at every turn one sees "a plaque with an epitaph or a crucifix at a road junction. You can't avoid them. [. . .] The people have been walled in with graves, [. . .] and they fatten themselves on the slime of the past" (78). In her discussion of Polish nationalism, Geneviève Zubrzycki sees "the cross as a dominant symbol and martyrdom as a core narrative" (2006, 34) in the creation of Polish national identity. The narrator sees in these roadside crosses constant reminders of historical tragedies, and the nationalist morality of obliging every citizen to suffer as Christ had. For the narrator this drive to celebrate martyrdom has created in Poland a cultural cemetery, in which suffering and a devotion to the past has become the most important commodity one can own. When describing the émigré Polish society of Belgium in "The Hunchback," Pankowski declares that "previous suffering is its treasure" (1993, 161).

Despite this critical view of Poland, the narrator defends the notion of fighting for Culture, and Society. He describes reading about the Spanish Civil War in the papers as a child. He tells Rudolf that "anyone who believed . . . in man was walking through mountains and forests, at night, like a robber! Across the Pyrenees so as to enlist under the standard of the International Brigades" (47). He assumes that it will be impossible for Rudolf to remain "apolitical" about this, as he had spent the War "hunting" young men and soldiers instead of fighting for the fascists. "Anyone who believes in man" must defend the International Brigades and celebrate their heroic sacrifices. Rudolf, however, replies:

> You were—please forgive me—just a kid who wanted to perform some exploit. I suppose the barricades were a party treat for youngsters in poor countries . . . where "heroism" comes easier than a pair of boots. There old fellows pushing fifty get the booze and the whores while kids' heads are stuffed with all and sundry who wear fetters like adornments. [. . .] My dear man! In Europe at that time, how many shouted "no pasaran"? Maybe a few hundred. [. . .] The rest lived *for themselves*. Please listen—because they had the right to live! And we in Paris had the right to live our lives without the seal of history on our naked, private arses! [. . .] My dear man—what is a body guilty of that first these, then those order it to impale itself on bayonets? Get them off my happiness! [. . .] *our lot* found themselves in this situation anyway . . . alongside the others from the barricades. You know very well the Hitlerites packed homosexuals off to concentration camps. But nothing is said about this today. (48–49)

Rudolf begins by trivializing the narrator's admiration of the International Brigades, suggesting he is stuck in an infantile fantasy of "performing some exploit." Despite the intentions of the cause, Rudolf sees in the narrator's naïve optimism the same Romantic, nationalist rhetoric of hero/martyr worship. In his cynicism he notes that those who did the dying and fighting were the young, "stuffed" with a petty idealism adorned with their own bondage, their suffering turning into a commodity. In his defense of "youth" he is once again privileging the life it represents over the death represented by "the old," who send the young to die. Once again, I must note the apparent influence of Gombrowicz here. This notion of "the old" sending "the young" to die in wars brings to mind my discussion of *TransAtlantyk* in chapter 1. Tomasz, the representative of Polish culture, manhood, and "ojczyzna," wishes to send his son Ignacy, the representative of youth, and "synczyzna," back to Europe to fight and probably die for Poland. Both Gonzalo and Rudolf side with youth and life, while "Gombrowicz" and Pankowski-the-narrator side with tradition and death.

Rudolf goes further in his criticism, suggesting it was probably poverty more than their idealism that drove these youths to fight, heroism being cheap. He defends one's right to live for oneself instead of dying for the imagined ideals of the heroic sacrifice for the many. He defends the rights of the body, of keeping one's "private arse" safe. For Rudolf it does not matter on which side of a conflict "these and those" who give the commands are. They are all representatives of the cult of death that he opposes. In demanding the sacrifice "on the barricades" they are denying the importance of the body, relegating it to a status beneath an intangible idealism. They wish to subjugate the unruly body so it can serve a certain principle—honor, martyrdom, the nation. He rejects the martyrological value of these actions and once again takes the side of life and living for oneself. He is appalled by the opposing notion of dying for your nation. Instead of rejoicing in the sacrificial act of throwing oneself onto bayonets, Rudolf would rather rejoice in his happiness, a happiness he sees as constantly threatened by the patriotic fervor of "these and those."

Rudolf then articulates a rare expression of community, claiming membership in "our lot," that is gay people. It seems that if he had to, the only "nation" he would wish to be a part of would be a "queer nation." This sentiment is truly compelling. In the Introduction I discuss Lauren Berlant and Elizabeth Freeman's essay "Queer Nationality," which analyzes the radical, direct-action group Queer Nation. They illustrate that in miming "the privileges of normality" the group "stimulate[s] 'the national' with a camp inflection" (1993, 196). Their parody of the nation-state "exploits the symbolic designs of mass and national culture in order to dismantle the standardizing apparatus that organizes all manner of sexual practice into 'facts' of sexual *identity*" (196). They re-articulate nationalist and heteronormative rhetoric but with a "camp" bent in order to destabilize these values. When Rudolf claims allegiance to a queer nation he denies the nineteenth-century iteration of the nation-state, an act that subverts its monolithic status. He finishes by mentioning the suffering this community had endured at the hands of the Nazis, along with those "from the barricades." It is the only instance in which he comments on the suffering of "his people." In refusing to take part in the martyrological drive, despite the oppression experienced by his queer nation, he rejects the power of martyrology as expressed by others.

In a later exchange near the end of the story Rudolf returns to his condemnation of sacrifice and his defense of the body:

> All our heads have been inoculated with this cult of public mutilation and death on the barricades . . . and so on from generation to generation. It's reached a point where the head, drunk with heroic hysteria, gazes "with pride" and "with self-denial" . . . at the despair of the body that nourishes it. . . . So that when the body falls, the head's still reciting a select number of little verses, you know, that force you to stand to attention automatically. (93)

According to Rudolf, we have been convinced to take a masochistic pride in our denial of the body and our worship of "the head," or rather the logos. We have become disgusted by the very necessity of the body in survival. We have been systematically programmed to die and kill for "little verses" that hold some kind of patriotic meaning. It is in this "heroic hysteria" and the demand for "public mutilation" that Rudolf sees the fraudulence of Society and Culture's claims of superiority over the Individual and Jouissance. In his fight for "an existence filled with physical enjoyment and abundant love" (De Bruyn et al., 2011, 471), Rudolf must oppose these messianic systems of control and regulation. It is against Society and Culture that Rudolf defends "the body's freedom," its "right to reach for happiness" (94).

Near the end of the novella the narrator describes going to visit Rudolf's grave. He is surprised to discover that Rudolf had been married, and even had a son he named Olek.[7] When he reaches the grave the narrator kneels and writes "Yazit" in the sand (105). It is a simple gesture, but one that implies the narrator has in some measure reconciled with Rudolf. It is perhaps too much to suggest that this gesture indicates that the narrator has adopted or even accepted Rudolf's morality of jouissance and his rejection of the morality of self-denial and sacrifice. However, in rewriting the name of one of Rudolf's great loves, a name that had been scrawled across his belly, the narrator has certainly been opened to other possibilities of life and love.

CONCLUSION

After moving from poetry and drama to prose, Marian Pankowski's writing took on a decidedly political character. Often through parody and satire, it questioned received notions of what constituted Polish identity. In his engagement with the Romantics, he undermined the power of their nationalism and messianic morality of sacrifice and suffering. As Janusz Termer notes, "He is perceived as a relentless critic of 'national holiness' and various hardened native myths, an irreverent iconoclast of traditional customs and unmindful religious sentiments" (2009, 69). While early critics saw this as little more than sophomoric, and unpatriotic, I would argue that it is a complex, and truly patriotic project. His criticisms are ultimately productive: they act as a mirror put up to Poland's face, forcing it to reflect on the value of the heteronormative and nationalist ideologies that have led the nation into a morality of masochism and the beautiful death (*la belle morte*). Through his "pounding against the national literature" Pankowski wishes to reveal to Polish society its superstitious, stubborn reliance on out-of-date customs, and its self-destructive messianic nationalism. *Rudolf,* more than any of his other works, successfully achieves this. In its critical interrogation of Polish values, its undermining of Romanticism's messianic mythos, and its unapologetic use of queer erotics, *Rudolf* remains one of the most challenging works of modern Polish fiction.

NOTES

1. This tactic has proven successful by other Central European authors, such as the Czech writer Milan Kundera who now writes in French first.
2. See Genevieve Zubrzycki (2006).
3. See chapter 1.
4. All English-language citations from *Rudolf* for this essay refer to Marian Pankowski (1996). For Polish-language citations, I used Marian Pankowski (1984).
5. See chapter 1, for my discussion of *The Teacher* and *TransAtlantyk*.
6. In the original Polish Pankowski differentiates between "*przekroczyć*," "to cross," and "*wykroczyć*," "to trespass."
7. One must note the misogyny apparent in the description of Rudolf's wife. This is undoubtedly an important aspect of the story; however, it does not entirely fit in the goals of my project here. For an excellent feminist analysis of women characters in Pankowski's fiction see Inga Iwasiów (2011).

Chapter Four

Olga Tokarczuk

Transgressive Bodies, Transgressing Borders

In the preceding three chapters, every author I have discussed had to contend with the reality of the Polish communist state at some point in their career. While Jarosław Iwaszkiewicz actually lived quite comfortably under the system—as president of the Polish Writers' Union he was a mid-level *apparatchik* in the Polish communist government—the influence of his sexuality on his work was a topic no one could have broached. This demand to keep hidden one's non-normative sexuality is illustrated further in the work of Julian Stryjkowski, who had to couch his discussions of the homoerotic in the five-hundred-year-old story of Michelangelo. It is no wonder then that the most open discussions of homoeroticism from the time would come from two authors who were living abroad, and therefore not subject to the demands of the Polish United Workers' Party (PZPR). Neither Witold Gombrowicz's nor Marian Pankowski's works were immediately welcomed in the Polish People's Republic (PRL), *TransAtlantyk* being published by the exile press Instytut Literacki in Paris, and *Rudolf* not even being published in the Polish language until four years after its first appearance.[1]

With the fall of communism in 1989, state enforced censorship ended. However, with the downfall of communism, Poland witnessed a resurgence of right-wing, nationalist ideology in both the political and social spheres. Justyna Sempruch sees the 1990s as a period of a "post-communist revival of patriarchy in Poland," a time of "an increasing masculinization of power structures" that saw the criminalization of abortion and an official "discouraging" of contraception and divorce (2008b, 2). She also notes a "return to social policies based on marriage and the family as primary paradigms of women's identities" (2). One author of the post-socialist era whose work has contested this swing to the right is Olga Tokarczuk. In this chapter I analyze three novels that make up her "Silesian Trilogy" written during the last decade of the twentieth century; *E. E.* (1995), *Longago and Other Times* (2004), and *House of Day, House of Night* (1998). In these novels Tokarczuk first uses a feminist deconstructive methodology and later a queer post-modern aesthetic in order to subvert notions of stable borders between nations, genders, and ethnicities. The contested geographical space of Silesia (*Śląsk*) becomes a leitmotif of the fluidity and porous character of such borders. Sempruch calls this area of Poland "a nationally ambivalent territory," one that is "placed in-between geographically 'authentic' and imaginary spaces" that fuses "culturally different historical traces" (2008b, 4). This is an especially important theme in the historical context of the post-socialist 1990s, during which the nations of Central and Eastern Europe once again went through a period of instability and transformation.

Tokarczuk is one of the most celebrated living authors of contemporary Polish literature.[2] She has won several literary awards, including becoming the first Polish winner of the Man Booker Prize in 2018, and has been shortlisted for the prize in 2019. She is also a two-time winner of the Nike, one of the most prestigious awards for Polish literature. Most recently, and most notably, she won the 2018 Nobel Prize in Literature, becoming the sixth Polish author to do so. Well before this achievement, Philip Marsden had already placed her among two other Polish Nobel laureates, Czesław Miłosz and Wisława Szymborska, in his review of her novel *House of Day, House of Night* (2002). According to Kazimiera Szczuka, Tokarczuk represents "the most important contemporary myth-writer, searching for literary images of religious, unconscious and archetypal structures in spaces of 'minor' and borderline plot" (2000, 69). Aside from her literary output she has been engaged in critical scholarly work as well. Her book *The Doll and the Pearl* (2000) drew the ire of the Polish academic world for daring to re-analyze Bolesław Prus's classic *The Doll* (1890). In recent years, she has repeatedly been the target of similarly reactionary criticism. In 2015 she was attacked by the "Nowa Ruda Patriots Association," a nationalist organization from her adopted home town in southwestern Poland. Waldemar Bonkowski, a senator of the right-wing Law and Justice Party (PiS) demanded that her honorary citizenship of the city be rescinded for maligning Polish history and culture to the rest of the world (Piekarska 2015b). Tokarczuk fired back that indeed she is the true patriot, not nationalists who promote racism and homophobia (Piekarska 2015a). Quite recently, when asked what he thought about Tokarczuk winning such a prestigious award like the Man Booker, Vice Prime Minister Piotr Gliński—another member of PiS—said, "It would be good if she were a reasonable Polish writer who understood Polish society and the Polish community" (Karpiuk 2019). What he sees as "unreasonable" in Tokarczuk's writings is her insistence on revealing the truth about Poland, whether that truth shows Poland in a positive or negative light. Despite the fame such awards bring to Polish letters, nationalists simply cannot abide any criticism of the nation. To allow such critique would be to admit that the nation and their national identity rests on unsure ground.

Tokarczuk has also been deeply concerned with issues of feminism and theoretical ideas on identity formations. In an interview with Stanisław Bereś, she stated:

> Writing is an experiment with identity. I've been playing with the vague concept or hypothesis that we are each many people, that there are many of us in one body, and that living depends on, among other things, an examination of all our possible selves. [. . .] We have at our disposal an entire repertoire of roles, and unfortunately the process of our maturation depends on the fact that we start to restrict ourselves to the most tried and tested expression of the self. (qtd. in Bereś 2002, 495)

Tokarczuk's ideas on the processes of identification echo many of those expressed by queer theorists in the west. In 2008 a Polish translation of Judith Butler's *Gender Trouble* (1990) (Uwikłani w płeć) finally appeared (Tokarczuk 2008). Interestingly, Tokarczuk herself wrote the introduction to the translation, saying that *Gender Trouble* "has become, over the last few years a fundamental source text not only for feminism, but also for thinking on the foundations of culture" (2008, 5). These and other examples illustrate Tokarczuk's engagement with both feminism and queer theory. In this context her novels become a forum for minority voices that resist heteronormative power structures of nationalism and patriarchy.

All three novels of Tokarczuk's "Silesian Trilogy" adhere to a postmodern aesthetic, in both structural and thematic terms. One common feature they share involves the very physical form of the books themselves. The first edition of *Houses* included a bookmark with a recipe for poisonous mushrooms, which is found in one of the stories of the novel. Inside *E. E.* there is a business card for a haberdashery owned by "Erna Eltzner," the main character of the novel, who ends up owning a hat shop at the end of the story. *Longago and Other Times* includes a bookplate illustrated with a phoenix, with "Ex Libris" written on it, precisely matching bookplates that are pasted into books as described within the story. These additions clearly illustrate Tokarczuk's concern with undermining borders, each being a transgressive, postmodern play with notions of boundaries. Through them she attempts to break down the barrier between the story and the audience, suggesting that the story exceeds the artificial limits of the book itself. For Tokarczuk there is an interpenetration between life and art. These seemingly trivial quirks of the books' production are potent symbols of border crossings that prove important throughout Tokarczuk's work. Ewa Wampuszyc sees in Tokarczuk's work a move to undermine "dominant cultural narratives," by "unmasking their instability, rather than simply idealizing a place or past." It undermines "dominant discourses of Polish culture," especially around the nationalist myth of the "Recovered Territories" of western Poland, particularly Silesia (2014, 368, 381).[3] In my analysis of these novels, I show that through her play with such transgressivity, Tokarczuk engages in a move to destabilize nationalist regimes of patriarchy and heteronormativity, ultimately hoping to open Polish culture up to more acceptance of difference.

ERNA

E. E. is the story of Erna Eltzner, a young girl of Polish and German parentage, growing up in turn of the century Breslau, which will be renamed Wrocław less than twenty years later. The story follows Erna as she gains the ability to see and communicate with the dead, and acts as a medium during séances for various family friends. She begins taking lessons on spiritism from Walter Frommer, whose sister Teresa once had the same abilities. She also attracts the attention of Artur Schatzmann, a student of psychiatry who decides to write a study about her for his doctoral project.

In its wish to preserve a stable homogeneity, nationalism desires an adherence to heterosexist norms, and demands the maintenance of male privilege. Similarly to the queer male body, the female body is too open to penetration and therefore to pollution to be entrusted as the national body.[4] The patriarchy, therefore, must maintain control of national discourse in order to maintain the closed male body as the national body. Erna's gift begins to shift this privilege away from the patriarchy, and so destabilizes its control over the nation.

The novel begins with Erna seeing a ghost and then losing consciousness. She talks about her vision with her mother, who believes her without question. When a German doctor comes to see Erna he calls her mother's—Mrs. Eltzner's—claims of Erna's new abilities "*bzdura*." This same word, "nonsense," is repeated later by Mr. Eltzner, who, after Mrs. Eltzner relates Erna's vision to him, says, "That's the quickest way to turn her into a lunatic" (17). This sets up a tension between the rational German patriarchy and the irrational Polish matriarchy. After Mr. Eltzner dismisses her convictions, Mrs. Eltzner suffers an attack:

> Once again in her life she felt disillusioned and cheated. She was imprisoned in a house with a man who completely didn't understand her, as if they were from another world, as if they spoke different languages. She glanced at the decorated oak wall. She had the sensation that she was suffocating. She needed to leave there immediately, from that room, from that house. She felt a hatred that choked her. She made for the door clutching at her throat. From the depths of her body she felt the throbbing of some enormous wave. Stunned by this

din, she began to stagger. She wanted to take a strong deep breath, but her throat tightened and only a wheezing sound escaped. (17)

Her husband refuses Mrs. Eltzner's language, and so her body must try to speak for her. The word is the domain of the father, and is therefore denied to the mother, who must remain mute and attempt to speak bodily only. However, since the word—the rational—is privileged over the body—the irrational—the mother is refused any language at all. Justyna Sempruch calls this an act of hystericizing "the unheard voice of the woman whose language is reduced to psychosomatic symptoms" (2008a, 2). This hystericizing of the feminine voice is an attempt to maintain the peripheral status of that voice. The scene presents several binaries that Tokarczuk subverts and deconstructs throughout the course of the novel. Mr. Eltzner, as the locus of authority and power in the family, is attributed with aspects such as rationality and the logical, which then in turn become equated with the German and masculine. He is contrasted with Mrs. Eltzner, through whom attributes such as the irrational and emotional are equated with the Polish and feminine. In each binary the site of privilege rests with those attributes designated as masculine. The stability of these binaries remains intact until the awakening of Erna's mediumistic abilities.

Before Erna gains her powers she barely seems to exist, possessing almost no kind of individuality. As one of the younger daughters she is awarded little status in the family. The attention her older sisters receive is born almost solely from the fact that they are of marrying age. The story also describes how her brothers, though younger, have a much higher status in the family hierarchy. Her father is depicted as loving his children "in general." Mrs. Eltzner must continually remind him of their names, except for those of his two sons, whom he obviously favors. That her father pays so little attention to her is especially important in the context of her identity formation. In her reading of the novel, Urszula Chowaniec notes that it is her father's gaze "that is constitutive for her existence" (2010, 158). In such a patriarchal system one's identity flows strictly from the acknowledgement of the holder of authority, namely the father. Even her mother describes Erna as "shy, ugly, lonely, and strange to the world, as if she didn't belong in it" (13). She describes her other children as "athletic," "serious," "coquettish" and "self-sure." Unlike her siblings, Erna occupies a non-presence that is recorded later by Artur Schatzmann when he first meets her: "First impression from direct contact with E. E. is her absentmindedness, her 'absence'" (208). Through Erna, "absence" becomes tied to the feminine, equating "presence" to the masculine, which reinforces the privilege of the patriarchy. Erna's insubstantiality changes once people recognize her supernatural abilities. The first time Walter Frommer comes to meet with Erna to discuss spiritism it seems to him that "in a sense he was seeing her for the first time" (32), even though he had been a family friend for years prior. Similarly to Mr. Eltzner, Frommer had always seen the Eltzner children "as a whole," or one "single organism." For him, "Erna did not have her own existence. [. . .] He realized that she had never existed for him as a person. He had to see her anew" (33). Ironically, at the same time Erna becomes more substantial for other people, her self-identification becomes more fluid. During her first séance she feels as though she is not someone "who feels, thinks or perceives, she was now something completely without borders. She could not even die, because she had been spread out beyond life, beyond death and beyond time" (43). There remains no "'proper boundary' between her soul [which could be understood as the *unconscious*] and her physical body" (Sempruch 2008a, 110). While her external identity coalesces, her consciousness takes on a more liminal character.

Hélène Cixous's theory of *écriture feminine* is an excellent tool in demonstrating the way in which Tokarczuk here disrupts classic male/female binaries as illustrated in the hybrid character of Erna. The liminality of Erna's identity is in conflict with patriarchal ideologies that wish all identity to be fixed and clear. According to Morag Shiach, Hélène Cixous's project attempts "to subvert the discourse of patriarchy, to open it up to contradiction and to difference" (1991, 20). *Écriture feminine* is not an attempt simply to replace the privilege of a "male writing" by privileging a "female writing." Rather, it is a deconstructive move aimed at reducing the privilege of logocentricism and rejecting essentialism in order to give more voice to pluralistic approaches. *Écriture feminine* happens in the "'between,' in that space which is uncertain, dangerous in its refusal to ally itself with one side of an opposition. Stepping outside, negotiating the between, feminine writing is to carve out a new space of representation that will not fit into old grids" (Shiach 1991, 22). The unquestioned authority of Mr. Eltzner, especially in determining Erna's identity, is an example of one of these "old grids." When Erna becomes a medium, endowed with a certain amount of power, an identity all her own begins to form that is, for the first time, not determined by her father. Urszula Chowaniec sees this gift as situating "Erna far from the domain of the rational father" (2010, 158). Erna's gift begins shifting the unchallenged privilege of patriarchy, undermining the various binaries that before had been present. The adult characters who had previously barely acknowledged her existence, now look to her, and to her new language for guidance.

For Chowaniec the séances are no more than a means for other characters to exploit Erna, saying, "[n]o one seems to pay attention to her bodily suffering. The adults are curious only about the other world, and for them this is enough to justify Erna's sufferings" (2010, 159). While it is true that Erna's body is weakened through her communion with the spirit world, I would disagree with Chowaniec that this is simply yet another example of the female body being dominated and exploited. The only language allowed to Erna is that of her body, similarly to her mother as illustrated in the earlier passage. However, unlike her mother she gains authority through her abilities. Erna's realization of more of her power is in direct proportion to her growing awareness of her body. In *The Laugh of the Medusa*, Hélène Cixous says the following about *écriture féminine*:

> Listen to a woman speak at a public gathering (if she hasn"t painfully lost her wind). She doesn't "speak," she throws her trembling body forward; she lets go of herself, she flies; all of her passes into her voice, and it's with her body that she vitally supports the "logic" of her speech. Her flesh speaks true. She lays herself bare. In fact, she physically materializes what she's thinking; she signifies it with her body. In a certain way she inscribes what she's saying, because she doesn't deny her drives the intractable and impassioned part they have in speaking. Her speech, even when "theoretical" or political, is never simple or linear or "objectified," generalized: she draws her story into history. (1976, 881)

Erna comes to exemplify Cixous's ideas about woman's language. Whereas earlier her mother's "bodily language" was unable to challenge the logocentrism of Mr. Eltzner's speech, instead staggering and succumbing to her "throat tightening," Erna's body takes on an authoritative role in her new language. Before her first séance she notices while looking at herself in a mirror that just below her navel "there appeared several dark hairs" (36). At the same moment she begins puberty, crossing the boundary from girl to woman, her mediumistic powers emerge, her body taking on a central role in her newfound language and identity formation. Cixous's ideas are analogous to Erna's position as spiritual medium. The society in which Erna finds herself is highly patriarchal and hierarchical. As medium her language becomes a hybrid between a cerebral and a bodily language. It is this hybridity that becomes the ultimate destabilizing force of binary systems of privilege. Gloria Anzaldúa notes that within patriarchal societies, where "culture is made by those in power—men," the very term "culture" itself comes to be read as "male" (1987, 38–39). Every component of culture, including language, is then the domain of the masculine. Erna-as-authority begins to complicate this equation.

Erna's abilities as a medium are made possible precisely through her hybridity. In the universe of the novel, being a woman is one of two prerequisites to gaining the abilities of a medium, the other being the possession of some kind of hybrid "ethnicity." These qualities are also found in the characters of Walter and Teresa Frommer. Their parents were a "Prussian doctor, diplomat, and traveler, a highly unusual person, and Anne-Marie von Hochenburg, a Silesian aristocrat" (24). What is more, their early lives were ones of constant flux and instability; Teresa being born in Morocco and

Walter in Mexico during their parents' unending travels. Later their mother leaves the father to be with a hypnotherapist in New York, but finally kills herself on the eve of their return to Europe. Walter and Teresa move into their grandmother's palace and become close with their cousin, Rainer, who begins to teach them how to hold séances. Through his tutelage Teresa begins to discover her abilities as a medium; however, Rainer seduces Teresa, after which he cuts off contact with them, and Teresa's abilities disappear. From that point on Teresa is only partially able to communicate with the supernatural world, and only while she is dreaming.

Like Erna, Walter and his sister have a hybrid ethnic identity that is made even more unstable by their experiences early in life. As a woman with such a background Teresa was once endowed with paranormal abilities similar to Erna's. Walter, on the other hand, being a man, is unable to communicate with the supernatural despite his deep interest in spiritism. However, since he is of a hybrid ethnic background, he is able to gain some insight from it, but only by being near his sister while she is dreaming:

> Only when his crippled and silent sister had sat next to Frommer with her knitting in her hands did something begin to happen. The rustling of the cards and the muttering of her brother must have overpowered her, because after a moment she would stop moving, close her eyes, and doze off to sleep. Now it seemed to Frommer that the writing and the cards began to take on some kind of sense. Strange associations would begin appearing in his head, thoughts from out of nowhere, suggestive images, and full of life. He allowed them to flow through his mind, savoring them disinterestedly, like someone who had happened upon a free ticket to a show. (21)

The suggestion then is that unlike the logocentric language of patriarchy, which refuses the participation of women, the hybrid language of the medium is somewhat open to both women and men. While Mrs. Eltzner had earlier been refused language in the presence of the *Father*, Frommer is allowed access to this new language in the presence of the *Mother*.

Cixous wrote of herself as inhabiting a hybrid identity, as being "heterogeneous, as made up of various identities, of many and varied desires" (Shiach 1991, 25). Similarly, Erna is herself a hybrid, having a Polish mother and German father. Like Erna's new language, Cixous's *écriture féminine* goes "outside narrative structures" to "create subjectivities that are plural and shifting" (22). Cixous illustrates that "it is impossible to sustain the complete dichotomy between mind and body which offers the illusion of intellectual control at the cost of erasing, censoring, and hystericizing the body" (70). The preservation of the mind/body binary is central to patriarchy maintaining both rhetorical and therefore, ideally, real control over the nation. Erna-as-medium acts as a destabilizing force that threatens to undermine this binary and in so doing to undermine patriarchal hegemony. As Erna's powers develop so too does her liminal existence. In describing the way she looks at things it appears as though she looks "somewhere to the side, the outline, the edge, the border between the object and the background, as though she wasn't interested in the thing itself but what was beyond it" (59). It is within this "between," this liminal space that Erna's identity begins to take shape independently of anyone else.

Eventually, she even comes to understand the world around her in her own terms. While on a visit to the country, Erna notices the Odra River, or Oder in German. For her the river outside the city is something different. "Erna didn't think of it as 'Odra,' this was a different river than the Odra in the city that barges floated over. This one was named She, and she was alive, young, powerful and merciless" (183). As the historical borderline between the Germanic and the Slavic, the Odra, which is grammatically feminine in both languages, is analogous to Erna; hers a liminal, fluid body, the Odra a liminal, fluid space, both balancing between two worlds. She ascribes attributes of strength and power to "she," re-appropriating this masculine vocabulary for the feminine, further destabilizing male privilege. Eventually Erna's powers develop more, and she begins foreseeing future events. When this happens dream reality begins to take the place of actual reality, the borders between the two becoming more fluid.

> The night became crowded, and her dreams with their own reality became closer to actual reality. Her morning ablutions, the breakfast ritual, making the bed, the games with the doctor and the two-hour lessons brought her back to real life, but around noon the border between reality and dream would smooth over [. . .] Erna once again would have the impression that she had begun to sleep, and what she was looking at was a dreamy illusion. [. . .] Finally she had to wonder where she was and what was reality. (60)

For Sempruch, when Erna inhabits this liminal space, she is able to "synthesize binaries, polarities [. . .] 'incorporating' the experience/place in which voices/bodies speak" (2008a, 111). The distinctiveness between reality and dream, between voice and body become blurred. In blurring these distinctions between body and mind, all other differences, gendered, national, and others, become blurred as well, resulting in Erna undermining the very foundations of patriarchal power.

The séances attract the attention of Artur Schatzmann, who decides to take part in the meetings and to study Erna for his doctoral project. This becomes the titular "E. E." The use of Erna's initials as a title to a psychoanalytical study immediately references the work of Freud, of whom Schatzmann becomes a follower. The introduction of Artur creates a tension between him and Walter Frommer. Frommer represents tradition and the pre-twentieth-century world, while Schatzmann represents science and the modern world. When Artur's mother tells him about Erna and her first séance, his immediate reaction is to imagine what it would be like to study such a phenomenon scientifically. "His excited imagination began to create images of laboratories, workshops full of instruments for taking one's blood pressure and pulse to which mad girls would be harnessed, lecture halls filled with students, graphs written on the chalkboard" (65). Artur's instinct is to measure and study, to attempt to make rational the irrational, instead of accepting the possibility of the irrational. What's more, as a man of science of the late nineteenth and early twentieth centuries, he automatically ties the irrational to "mad," or hysterical women. This is further evidenced when he imagines the books he would need by Pierre Janet and Jean-Martin Charcot, both of whom were some of the first to theorize about women's hysteria. Indeed, the full title of Artur's study on Erna will be "A Study of the Case of a Hysterical Teenage Girl Who Speaks with Ghosts." Before Schatzmann even meets Erna his first impulse is to diagnose her with hysteria, making an illness of her new abilities.

Schatzmann's scientific intentions contrast sharply with those of Walter Frommer, who believes in Erna's abilities unquestioningly and decides to train her in being a medium. When he discovers that Schatzmann has instructed Erna to keep a dream journal, Frommer accuses him of "stealing" her dreams; however, he analyzes Erna's dreams as well, though attaching a more spiritual meaning to them. Ironically, both the representative of tradition and the representative of modernity use similar methods to "study" Erna. Ultimately their studying is in fact an attempt to control her and her powers, and to control the new hybrid language it represents. Curiously, both Frommer and Schatzmann recognize Erna's liminality. Schatzmann sees Erna as "balancing between two worlds," calling it a "dwoistność," or "double-existence." During one of their lessons Frommer explains to Erna that existence is actually no more than "udawanie," which can be translated as "a seeming" or "pretending," recalling a Butlerean notion of performativity. However, instead of acknowledging Erna's fluidity as something positive, Schatzmann's recognition of her "double-existence" is for him merely a symptom of her sickness, the result of hysteria. What is more, for Frommer the "seeming-ness" of existence is actually an expression of a religious Platonism in which the realm of the Forms are the "true" expression of existence and life is merely shadows of those Forms. Both wish to make her abilities rational to their own systems of logical understanding, and thereby maintain the patriarchal monopoly over language and bodies in an attempt to reinstate patriarchy as the normalizing force. Even before meeting Erna, Schatzman concludes that hers is merely another case of hysteria, seeing her as no more than an object for study, as well as a means to further his career. While Frommer might believe he has Erna's best interests in mind, he also sees her as no more than a means to his own ends. This is reflected earlier in the novel in his interactions with his sister. After her dream trances, during which Walter is able to commune somewhat with the spirit world, Teresa asks him upon waking, "What was that?" His reply is simply "Nothing." It is clear that though she no longer has complete command over her mediumistic powers, she remains aware of them to a certain extent. Frommer's decision not to tell his sister of the insights he is granted through her dreaming demonstrates his desire to control her and her power in the same way he wishes to control Erna. Despite their belief that they oppose one another, both Frommer and Schatzmann remain invested in the maintenance of the same patriarchal order.

The single male character who seems to have Erna's best interests in mind is Dr. Leo Löwe, another liminal character in the story. Born in the Kingdom of Poland that lasted from 1815–1818, he grew up with stories of dybuks, golems, angels, and "other strange and secret creations of God" (39). His very name references the famous Rabbi Löwe of the Prague Golem mythology. Dr. Löwe takes on a synthesizing role between Schatzmann and Frommer. The story describes Löwe's aversion to the term "hysteria," saying "that word flowed from his colleagues' lips when they tried to hide their confusion" (39). During a discussion with Frommer, Löwe says that he is "not interested in any Certainty with a capital C" (204). He goes on to say that the existence of a soul no longer seems possible to him, and that he has begun "more and more to sense a chaos in all of this" (205). For Löwe, the scientific world of Schatzmann has lost credibility with the invention of the all-encompassing diagnosis of hysteria, and the spiritual world of Frommer demands too much faith in order and certainty. His acceptance of the chaotic puts him in league with Erna's liminality, and her new hybrid language.

Both the setting of *E. E.* and the timing of its publication are symbolically important to Tokarczuk's project. The Breslau of the story will eventually become Wrocław. At the time of the novel it is a quite homogenous city—mostly German and Jewish. Erna as a Polish German is an auger of what the city will eventually turn into—a hybrid palimpsestic space, layered by several cultures. Erna is a child of the *fin-de-siècle*, born in the transition between centuries, which is a moment of transition to modernity as well. The various artistic and literary movements of the era promoted decadence and rebellion against tradition, while the height of mechanical modernity, the First World War, was less than twenty years away. Tokarczuk also inserts various markers of this transition within the narrative, such as Erna's father buying one of the first automobiles in Breslau, and her mother reading a book by Helena Blavatsky, a late nineteenth-century Russian-German feminist and occultist. Erna is herself a transitional figure, balancing between the rational and irrational, the German and the Polish.

Her story becomes symbolic for the Poland of the 1990s. *E. E.* was published in the midst of the post-socialist transition. Tokarczuk's play with these moments of transition is a useful method for her to open up Poland to flux and instability as opposed to the patriarchal and nationalistic adherence to stasis and rigidity that was on the rise in Poland post-1989. This move toward more nationalist, chauvinist social norms culminated when the conservative Law and Justice Party and their junior partners, the nationalist League of Polish Families (LPR), which came to power in Poland in 2000, maintained some measure of influence until 2007, and has unfortunately regained political power. Through the character of Erna, whose woman-ness and hybridity grant her both authority and destabilizing power, Tokarczuk's novel can be read as a feminist text that works to repudiate the growing nationalism of post-socialist Poland. According to Tokarczuk, *E. E.* is about "cognitive vulnerability and about how we handle ourselves in our own rigid convictions, which blind us and demand we see reality from only one side, while the truth is always complex, and often internally contradictory" (qtd. in Bereś 2002). Like Cixous, Tokarczuk wishes to engage in a project of dismantling this "reality from only one side."

LONGAGO

The second book in Tokarczuk's Silesian Trilogy, *Longago and Other Times*, presents a world in which all borders are mere fantasies; as such, one does not necessarily transgress them, as there is no real limit to cross, subtly undermining received ideas about the tangible reality of borders. The novel revolves around the near-century-long, generational story of the Niebieski (Blue) family. It is also the history of twentieth-century Poland, beginning with the outbreak of World War One in 1914, through its twenty-year era of regained independence, through the Holocaust and World War Two, the communist era, and ending with the Solidarity movement of the 1980s. This history, however, despite the grand scale of it, is told in miniature, as it is only related through its effect on the small area the narrator defines as the town and region of Longago. The narrator takes great pains to describe the borders as having hard edges and well-defined limits: "To walk through Longago quickly, from north to south would take an hour. It takes just as long from east to west. If someone wanted to walk around Longago slowly, carefully examining everything, it would take an entire day, from morning to evening" (2004, 12).[5] Space, then, is measured in temporal terms, not in miles or kilometers, calling into question the actual precision of the measurement. Each side of Longago is guarded by one of four angels, adding a mythological element to the story. The narrator also references three places, Kielce, Taszów, and Jeszkotle—making the setting of Silesia—to better describe the geographical position of the town and area. However, while these three cities actually exist in Poland, there is no such place as Longago (*Prawiek*). The narrator says that it lies in the "center of the Universe" (12). The irony is that, cosmologically, no place is at the center of the universe, because every point is the center. This means that Longago is "everywhere and nowhere" simultaneously (Wampuszyc 2014, 370). Taken together, the use of time to measure space, the introduction of mythological elements, and the mixing of reality and fantasy create an ambiguity that will come to define the entire narrative, leaving the reader on unstable ground. The vagueness of the title itself lends to the novel's ambiguity, implying that it does not take place at any certain time, but rather in some previous, undefined time.

This tension between ambiguity and certainty reappears throughout the story. At one point, the borders of Longago are defined in even stricter terms, though taking on a magical quality. Ruta, the daughter of a witch-like character named Kłoska, decides to reveal the secret of the border to her friend Izydor. She takes him to a spot and says, "Here everything ends" (80), explaining that nothing exists beyond this point, that places he believes to exist in the world are not real, that when people leave they only dream that they have gone to other places but actually stand motionless at the border, eventually returning, taking "their dreams for memories of their trip" (81). The entirety of reality sits in the day-long walk one can take around Longago. Izydor reaches out and feels as though he is splitting into two people, his hands disappearing into the void of the border where existence ends. Ruta explains that when strangers appear in Longago it is because the border "knows how to give birth to ready-made people, and it seems to us that they have come from somewhere" (81). This is reaffirmed at the end of the novel, when Adelka, the granddaughter of the Niebieskis, "returns" home to Longago. Getting off the bus she has "the feeling that she had just woken up. She felt that she had been asleep, dreaming about her life in some town, with some people, amid confused and vague events" (174). In the universe of the story, this magical border is real. The narrator makes it quite clear that nothing exists on the other side. And yet, despite its reality as a border that delimits reality, marking it off from unreality, the "unreal" continually transgresses it. There is no point in the story when the events of the twentieth century do not affect Longago. At the beginning, men are taken away to fight during World War One; later, Nazis invade and murder the Jewish population, and are then driven back by the Red Army; at the end, the fortunes of certain characters are affected by the ruling Communist Party of Poland. Even though there is no outside to Longago, the outside constantly intrudes upon it.

This magical geography is made even stranger later on when Ruta shows Izydor the center of Longago, which is then, for the novel, the precise center of the universe. She brings him to a stone obelisk standing in the forest with what appears to be a hat on top of a face. Izydor realizes that it is multiple faces, one facing him and two others in profile. He begins running around the monument, but is only ever able to see the face turned toward him. Seeing this, he comes to the realization that "one cannot comprehend everything at once" (118). What the narrator is describing is a classic, four-faced statue of the Slavic god Sviatovid (Światowid in Polish). This is the first of two moments when the line between mythology and reality blurs. The second occurs later when Ruta decides to marry and leave for the city. Kłoska only agrees to the marriage if Ukleja, the husband, will let her return from May to September, he getting to have her from October to April (121). This references the myth of Demeter, Persephone, and Hades, a story explaining the cycle of seasons. The narrator's use of these myths is not done allegorically. Kłoska does not reference the myth in her demand; as a woman who lives in communion with nature, she is Demeter. Her connection to the natural world had already been punctuated when, earlier in the novel, she makes love to an angelica plant that had grown and bloomed in her front yard (49–50). Indeed, Ruta is the offspring of this union, clearly marking her as a stand-in for Persephone, a goddess of vegetation.

This transgression of the borders of the human also occurs with the animal in the stories of the Bad Man and Florentynka. The unnamed Bad Man had been a resident of Longago until he murdered somebody, went mad, and ran off into the woods to hide. He stays away from civilization for so long that he "was not himself, and he even forgot what it meant to be oneself" (24). Eventually his life in the woods away from humanity begins to change him. He grows thick hair all over his body, he begins running on all fours, and his teeth and nails grow sharper, coming to resemble a dog more than a man. It does not take much for the human to fall away, for the line between person and animal to disappear. Florentynka also goes insane after years of tragedy, including the deaths of her husband and seven of her nine children. As an old woman, she begins talking at the moon, blaming it for her misfortunes. Then suddenly she gains the ability to communicate with animals. "The conversations depended on the sending of pictures. What the animals imagined was neither well developed nor concrete, unlike human speech" (44). There is no note in the text that Florentynka only believes she is communicating with animals because of her madness, though her illness has made it possible. The loss of her sanity has made the borders of her self more porous, allowing her a closer connection to the animal world.

Ewa Wampuszyc sees the central theme of *Longago* as the "transgression of borders, time, space and the empirically knowable" (2014, 367). In Longago, all borders are suspect, whether they be the borders of a geopolitical space, the borders between humans, animals, and plants, or even the borders between reality and myth.

HOUSES

In her later, and much more well-known novel, *House of Day House of Night*, Tokarczuk makes greater use of her postmodern play with transgressivity. Unlike *E. E.* and *Longago*, which adhere to strictly linear plots, *Houses*' structure is quite loose and unbounded, illustrating a resistance to traditional ideas of form. The plot moves about temporally, geographically, and thematically. Though the main story is of the narrator, who has moved to a small Silesian town outside Nowa Ruda, each chapter or section is either a story in itself or a piece of a larger story that runs throughout the text.

In its desire for a homogeneous space, nationalist discourse demands stable gender constructions. However, the narrator of *Houses* begins the novel with a dream that opens a space for considering the fluidity of identity. "The first night I had an unmoving dream. I dreamt that I was pure seeing, pure vision and I had neither a body nor a name [. . .] nothing belonged to me, because I didn't even belong to myself, and there wasn't even anything like 'I'" (7). Within the dream the narrator is both bodiless and nameless, subverting the entire category of the ego. In such a state "belonging" and "ownership" of an identity are impossible. The very notion of a stable mode of identification is itself suspect, as the speaker cannot even identify him/herself as "I." Instead, "I" becomes a disembodied, floating signifier, which remains impossible to define. In describing the dream further, she realizes that she can see through everything, noticing sleeping people who only "seemingly" remain still:

> None of these dreaming bodies were closer or farther from me. I looked at them, and in their tangled, dreamlike thoughts I saw myself—then I discovered a strange truth. That I am simply vision, without reflection, without any value, without emotion. And immediately I discover something else—that I am able also to look through time, that just as I can change my point of view in space, I can change it in time as well, *as if I were* a cursor on a computer screen that moves on its own, or simply doesn't know about the existence of the hand that moves it.[6] (7)

With no ego the narrator is unbounded, and is therefore able to see herself in other people. She is not a person; she is "simply vision," untied to predetermined systems of identification. Perhaps the most intriguing point in this opening scene comes when the narrator, in describing the point of view from which she is watching this dream, says "I can also change it in time, *as if I were* a cursor on a computer screen" (8). The significance of the Polish subjunctive structure used in this sentence is impossible to render into English. The best possible translation is the above "as if I were," for "jakbym było"; however, what is lost here is that Tokarczuk's narrator has expressed this statement in the neuter gender. In Polish, when one conjugates verbs in the past, the gender of the subject is also made evident. The fact that she has conjugated the verb "to be" ["być"] as "było," means that the subject of the sentence is neither feminine nor masculine, but effectively neuter.[7] We read here the "I am" of the narrator; however, even though the gendered grammar of Polish should inform the reader what the narrator's gender is, not only does the narrator deny this information, s/he purposely complicates the issue by using the neuter gender, which is grammatically impossible in Polish as implied subjects derive their gender from their biological gender. Curiously, at the beginning of the passage, the narrator says "mia*łam* nieruchomy sen" [I had an unmoving dream], in which the ending "-am" of "miałam" informs the reader that the narrator is indeed feminine. Thus, within the dream state, the narrator loses her gender. As Katarzyna Beilin notes, "The use of the neuter form of the verb may remind one of Blanchot's 'third *genre*' that contains the enigma lying between all binary opposites. It speaks from 'non-place,' which is the space of the Other, and it is a function of that which has no place" (2001, 451). When Tokarczuk creates the neuter "I," a genderless subject, the identity of the narrator becomes unbounded and unstable, open to a multivalent mode of gender identification.

Two stories from the novel that further illustrate Tokarczuk's concern with unbounded gender identifications are about Saint Kummernis and her biographer, a monk named Paschalis. Kummernis's biography is a "found text" that the narrator buys in a flea market bookshop, and is then placed inside the novel. She was born to a baron, and, as the author of the biography recounts, "she was born imperfect for her father [. . .] because her father wanted a son" (54). According to the dominant patriarchal order, Kummernis is the "wrong sex." She is imperfect because she cannot carry on the patriarchal lineage. After the baron marries off Kummernis's sisters, he sends her to a convent since she is too young to marry. After several years have passed, the baron demands that Kummernis marry one of his lords in order to make some kind of practical use of her. She refuses, however, saying that she is now married to Christ, and hides in a cave, where she performs various miracles. Her father, ignoring the importance of her miracle working, finally forces her to return home, where he locks her in a cell until she agrees to be married. As he tells her, "In body you belong to the world and you have no lord except me. [. . .] I am the master of your life, He is the master of your death" (58). In no aspect of her existence can Kummernis experience freedom. Her body belongs to the earthly patriarchy, and even in death she is subject to a religious, patriarchal order. After waiting several weeks, the baron suggests to the lord that he rape Kummernis so that she will have no choice but to marry him. However, when the young lord goes to Kummernis's cell, he finds that her face has been transformed into a man's, complete with beard, and now resembles Christ. In a rage, the baron crucifies Kummernis saying "since God is in you, then die like God" (68). Kummernis's transformation, especially in its hermaphroditic liminality, threatens her father's control over her. She finds herself a victim of the demands of a patriarchy, whose order must be maintained, through "family" violence if necessary.

The life of the character Paschalis, a young monk and Kummernis's biographer, also speaks to the instability of gender identity. His biography is quite similar to Kummernis's: "He was born somehow imperfect, because ever since he could remember he felt wrong inside, as though at birth he chose the wrong body, the wrong place, the wrong time" (74). Like Kummernis, he is born "imperfect"; however, unlike Kummernis, his imperfection is not the creation of any outside defining gaze, but instead comes from his own inner search for identity. When he enters the monastery and becomes a monk, he changes his name from Johann to Paschalis, but "despite the change of name, clothes, and even smells, Paschalis still felt uncomfortable inside himself" (75). He still does not feel as though he is himself, continuing to lack both identity and agency. He only begins to obtain subject-hood when he sees a painting of Mary, Jesus, and Saints Apollonia and Catharine. As he looks at the painting he imagines that he is in it:

> Paschalis was either St. Catharine or Saint Apollonia—he couldn't decide which. At any rate, he was one of them. He had long hair that flowed down his back. His dress tightly embraced his round breasts and fell to the Earth in delicate, wonderful waves. The naked skin of his legs felt the soft caresses of the material. (75–76)

Paschalis's male body, a system that the dominant patriarchal order wishes to be bounded, begins to open up. This opening up of his male body comes closer to fruition after he begins having an affair with another monk, Celestyn. As they carry on their relationship, Paschalis wonders more and more what it would be like to be a woman:

> He began to imagine that he himself was a woman. [. . .] The very idea of having a woman's body, with that secret hole between your legs, made him shudder with pleasure until it became an obsession. He wondered what such a thing might look like. [. . .] Paschalis would have given the world to know this sinful secret, but not in the usual way, from the outside, he wanted to live it, to experience it himself. (80)

In this passage, the narrator makes it clear that Paschalis does not wish to experience the female body "from the outside," as a man experiencing a woman. Rather he wishes that the female body were his own; he wishes to be a woman. Kummernis's transformation and Paschalis's desire to become a woman both illustrate Judith Butler's idea of the fluid nature of gender identity: "When the constructed status of gender is theorized as radically independent of sex, gender itself becomes a free–floating artifice, with the consequences that *man* and *masculine* might just as easily signify a female body as a male one, and *woman* and *feminine* a male body as a female one" (1990, 6). Both Kummernis's and Paschalis's genders become "free-floating artifices," unbounded by patriarchal demands.

When Celestyn dies Paschalis is left friendless. He travels to a nearby convent to deliver food and supplies, where he pretends to be sick so the other monks will leave him behind. He becomes close to the prioress, and begs her to allow him to stay in the convent, confessing his relationship with Celestyn, and his desire to be a woman, and telling her "about his body, which didn't want to be as it was" (83). The prioress eventually agrees. One night she takes him to a small chapel, and shows him a statue of the crucified Kummernis. The Prioress relates Kummernis's story to Paschalis, explaining that she is not yet a canonized saint, but that the nuns already recognize her as their patron. She tells Paschalis that she wants him to write Kummernis's biography, which he will then take to Rome to petition for her canonization. The prioress chooses Paschalis to write Kummernis's biography because she recognizes the similarity between them. She sees them both as examples of the instability of basing gender identity on sex, saying, "it is difficult to comprehend all of God's works" (83).

Paschalis agrees to write the biography, finishing it after several months, and then travels to the Glatz bishopric to present it and his petition for Kummernis's canonization to the Church authorities. When he is brought before a council of bishops, they tell him that though he has written the biography quite beautifully, there are some unnerving elements of the story that verge on heresy. One bishop offers him examples of women who offer ideal models of the female saint:

> Saint Agatha, who refused to marry the pagan king of Sicily, and instead cut off her breasts. Saint Catharine Aleksandryjska, who was torn apart by horses, or Apollonia, a pillar of faith in a time of persecution. They strapped her to a pole and pulled out her teeth one by one. Or Saint Fina, who was paralyzed, and strengthened her suffering by sleeping on the stone floor, until, finally, the rats ate her. (162)

The bishops' refusal to canonize Kummernis demonstrates how the gender transgressive body is even more subversive of the patriarchal order than the female body, a threat Kummernis's father had recognized earlier. Though the Church canonizes women, it does so only to praise the subservience of the feminine to the masculine. The image of the ideal martyred female body is one of mutilation and should only be praised in its degradation. Kummernis's body, however, is neither exclusively female nor male. In its transgression of gender boundaries, it is not subservient, but subversive. According to Val

Gough, in medieval Christianity certain aspects of Christ's gender construction were multivalent:

> If Christ's body in the Middle Ages was constructed erotically as the battered and bleeding beloved other, it was also imagined as a maternal body that nurtured and fed. Christ-as-mother nurtured through the bleeding wound in His side, which functioned symbolically like a lactating breast, and the bodies of women mystics—through healing blood and milk, for example—took on this maternal function in their own *imitatio Christi*. (2000, 240)

Similarly, Caroline Bynum points out that during the Middle Ages, "Both men and women described Christ's body in its suffering and its generativity as a birthing and lactating mother" (1987, 260–261). Later in the novel, this idea of "God-as-mother" is expressed in a passage Paschalis comes across in which Kummernis says, "God is a woman who is constantly giving birth. Lives pour from Her incessantly. There is no respite in this endless procreation. Such is the nature of God" (211). The bishops' refusal to canonize Kummernis reflects this paradigm and their fear that once the female is recognized in God and Christ, the hierarchy of the masculine over the feminine will completely dissolve. This, in turn, calls into question the entire power structure of the patriarchal order of the Church. It is therefore essential to this hegemonic order that gender remain a stable, bounded system. If the faithful exalted the crucified, transgressive body of Kummernis, exalting the female and male as one, there is no reason they would not also exalt the maternal female body of Christ.

After his failure, Paschalis begins to wander the streets of the city, eventually coming to a brothel. A young prostitute approaches, and takes him inside. As he lies on top of her, he is unsure what he should do. She tells him, "'There's something wrong with you.' [. . .] 'You're so beautiful, you've got hair like a woman'" (164). Like the prioress earlier, the young prostitute recognizes the instability Paschalis feels in the body of a man. He suddenly stands up, takes her dress, and puts it on. "He closed his eyes and ran his hands over his breasts and hips" (164). Then, still in the dress, "he sank on top of her slowly, and entered her without a mistake, as if he had practiced it a hundred times" (164). In this scene, Paschalis's use of drag demonstrates a "palimpsest of sexual identity"[8]—though covering himself in femininity, his masculinity continues to show through. Until he wears the dress, he cannot perform the sexual act with a woman. Although he destabilizes classic notions of gender identities by putting on the dress, he re-stabilizes his own identity through his act of cross-dressing. In her discussion of drag, Judith Butler notes that

> if the inner truth of gender is a fabrication and if a true gender is a fantasy instituted and inscribed on the surface of bodies, then it seems that genders can

be neither true nor false, but are only produced as the truth effects of a discourse of stable identity. [. . .] I would suggest as well that drag fully subverts the distinction between inner and outer psychic space and effectively mocks both the expressive model of gender and the notion of a true gender identity. (1990, 136–137)

Paschalis's simple act of putting on a woman's dress subverts any conception of stable gender identities to such a degree that there appears to be an actual physical change as in a seemingly magical-realist moment he "ran his hands over his breasts and hips."[9] Paschalis stays with Katka, the prostitute, rereading his biography of Kummernis. She brings him milk, telling him his breasts will grow if he drinks more. Finally, Paschalis comes to the realization that "he must create himself over again, this time out of nothing, because what he had been until now was based on the single misgiving that he had not been created properly, or perhaps that he had been created in a makeshift way, that he must destroy himself and arise again" (212). Paschalis has finally taken charge of the formulation of his self. He now understands the "mistake" of his birth, and has decided to remake himself in a better fitting identity. At the end of his work on Kummernis, Paschalis writes, "Please, whoever you are reading these words, remember the sinner Paschalis, a monk, who—were the Lord to grant him the possibility of a choice—would much more willingly choose the body of Kummernis, with all its sufferings and merits, than the honors of kingdoms" (68). It seems that Paschalis's prayer has been answered, as his body, similarly to Kummernis's has transgressed the borders of the male and the female.

Although Butler uses the term "free-floating artifice" to describe the fluid character of gender identity, the same term can be helpful in discussing national identity as well. Just as it becomes possible for man and masculine to signify a female body, "Poland" can signify an ethnically Polish, German, Ukrainian, or Czech body. Within this context Poland is a perfect illustration of the pliable, unbounded nation. Throughout its history, the geographical location that is now Poland has been Russian, Prussian, German, Austrian, Czech, and Polish. The setting of *Houses* is the Lower Silesian area of Poland, or Śląsk. Before World War Two, Śląsk had belonged to Germany for generations. Following Germany's defeat after the Second World War the Allies pushed its border several hundred miles west, placing Śląsk in Poland. As part of the process of claiming these areas, tens of thousands of German families were forced out. The area was then resettled by Polish families from Ukraine, Lithuania, and other parts of the eastern Polish borderlands, or *Kresy*.[10] The result of this process was a hybrid, palimpsestic space, no longer German, not really Polish, in a way "eastern," bordering on Bohemia and Germany. It is here that various national identities are forced to meet, and through their meeting a hybrid identity is created, being influenced by the "seepage" to the surface of past nations. At one point in *Houses*, Tokarczuk describes Nowa Ruda, the city in the center of this hybrid space. It is a town of

> crooked intersections, bypasses that lead to the centre, marketplaces on the outskirts, steps that start and finish on the same level, sharp turns that straighten roads, and forks where the left branch leads right, and the right branch left. [. . .] It's a town of fragments, a Silesian, Prussian, Czech, Austro–Hungarian and Polish town, a town on the periphery. (270)

The description here of Nowa Ruda stands in for a description of all of Śląsk. Tokarczuk attributes an almost magical nature to the region. It is a space where borders are constantly transgressed, a confusing space of paradoxes. This paradoxical character of Śląsk ultimately suggests that all orientation is disorientation. The fragmentary, palimpsestic construction of the region deconstructs the classic nationalist ideas of identity and reterritorializes it as an open, fluid space. As a fragmentary region, it takes on attributes of all the nationalities that have inhabited it, creating from them a new hybrid region. Just as the previous text of a palimpsest shows through a newer work written over it, influencing our view of it, so too do the various nations that have inhabited Śląsk show themselves. It is the existence of differences within a nation's borders that "constantly disturbs the myth of a unified people" (Branach-Kallas and Więckowska 2004, 7). We can call the people living in this area "Polish," but we must realize the arbitrary, constructed nature of that label.

One story from *Houses* that illustrates this is that of Peter Dieter, an ethnic German who had been raised in Silesia pre–World War Two. He and his wife decide to visit the region now in Poland where he was raised. His wife wants to see him the moment that he sees his old village, hoping that "she will finally understand all of Peter, from beginning to end, all his sadnesses [. . .] his stubborn patience, his wasting of time on foolishness, the risky way he passed cars on the highway and all the strange/foreign things that sat inside him that their forty years together hadn't changed" (92). Even though both Peter and his wife are "ethnically" German, his wife finds him to be strange or "foreign" (*obcy*). Unlike his wife, Peter is a Polish-German, or perhaps a German-Pole. Though the narrator never gives any specific details of his life, the implication is that he was one of several million ethnic Germans who were forced to leave Central and Eastern Europe after the Second World War. Simply by his presence in the novel, and especially his presence in Silesia, Peter Dieter's character demands the reader recognize the history of this region. He references the instability of national borders and of national identity. His "implied" life is one of displacement and exile. Though he is ethnically German, he feels his home to be Poland, or more precisely Silesia—which does not signify any legal, geopolitical space—and his wife also feels him to be "somewhat Polish." The question then is why can he not be considered Polish? The answer being, the vagaries of history and politics. Peter's character clearly illustrates the consequences of adhering to strict notions of stable national identities, constructions based on the exclusion of Others from a national discourse.

After travelling around Silesia, Peter and his wife finally come to his old village. He decides to walk up the low mountain alone until "he found himself on the very point where the border ran" (94). Suddenly, he finds it difficult to breathe. "He had one leg in Bohemia, the other in Poland. He sat there an hour, and second after second died" (95). Two Czech border guards eventually find his body. After thinking for a moment about the report they would have to write, they move his one leg from the Czech side to the Polish side. A half hour later two Polish border guards find him. After a moment's thought, "in solemn silence they took him by the arms and legs and moved him over to the Czech side" (95). Peter's entire life had been one of existing between borders, and his death is no different. He dies on an imaginary line, drawn by arbitrary means. Through their occupations, the Czech and Polish border guards physically embody the notion of discrete and separate nation-states. However, ironically, it is these same officials who seem to intuit the illusion of the ostensibly stable national borders they are paid to maintain. In order to avoid the headache of paperwork required to document the death, they simply transgress the invisible border between their nations, moving Peter's body from one side to another, ignoring the imaginary line. Through this simple act they illustrate the arbitrary, and therefore pliable character of national borders.

The fluidity and transgressivity of bodily and national borders coalesce later in the novel in two chapters entitled "She and He." These chapters tell the story of two unnamed people who number among the millions who were forced to immigrate to Silesia after the Second World War, while people like Peter Dieter were being removed. Their "foreignness" to the area is referenced several times as when the husband longs for his mother's Ukrainian cooking and the "warm Lviv accent" in which she spoke. The instability of the region is referenced by the German language on signs that still hang above shop windows, trains without timetables, and the other new residents who were difficult to understand as they all speak various regional dialects of Polish. They refer to their new home as being in a part of the country that is "no one's" (*niczyje*) (237). With the arrival of these new residents they have brought with them the Kresy of eastern Poland. Silesia, once homogenous, has now taken on the multivalent, porous character of the east. It has turned into a giant borderland with all the volatility that such regions possess. This sudden instability gives rise to two other characters, both named "Agni." The first Agni comes to the couple's home one day when the husband is away on business. The wife describes him as "otherworldly," and looking like a girl (241). The name itself is immediately curious as it does not comply with traditional Polish names for men, which almost always end with a consonant marking the word as grammatically masculine. Indeed it is the beginning of a common Polish woman's name—"Agnieszka." Agni does a day's worth of work for the wife, for which she gives him a meal and lets him sleep in the house. During the night he comes to her bedroom and they have sex, and he then suddenly leaves a few days later. The second Agni, this one a girl, comes to the home when the wife has gone to hospital for cancer treatment, and her husband remains alone in the house. He describes her as wearing trousers, and having a "boyish body" (253). When she tells him her name he replies, "From Agnieszka, right?" (246), but receives no reply. The husband, like his wife, begins an affair with this second, female Agni. When he asks her about herself Agni's reply is, "And who are you? [. . .] Where do you come from? Where are your parents?" (252). These questions, and Agni's refusal to answer them are telling. To know where one is from is central to knowing who one is, to beginning a process of identification. As a product of this unstable "no-place" of Silesia, Agni cannot say from where she/he is. His/Her plurality makes a concrete identity impossible, and instead she/he inhabits an unboundedness in much the same way the narrator does in the dream sequence from the beginning of the novel.

Tokarczuk's use of the name Agni for this, or perhaps "these" strange characters further accomplishes two things. First, just as a male Polish name usually ends in a consonant to reflect its masculine grammatical gender, most female Polish names usually end in an "a" to mark their feminine grammatical gender. The ambiguous nature of the name "Agni" is marked neither as a man's nor a woman's name in Polish, therefore leaving the holder of that name open to being either male or female. Second, the name also references the Hindu god "Agni" who had two faces, and was forever young and immortal. Both of these elements lead me to read Agni as a single, hermaphroditic character, who is able to change genders at will. Tokarczuk includes Agni not only to problematize ideologies of heteronormativity, but also to underscore further her view of Silesia's unstable national reality—an instability that creates an almost magical space that gives rise to such multivalent genders as those inhabited by Agni, Kummernis, and Paschalis.

In its description of the many "contested divisions and borders [. . .] between genders [. . .] and nations" (Bereś 2002, 502–503), *Houses* speaks to real world situations in Poland. Events from recent history, such as the previous conservative government's refusal to allow gay rights groups to march in Warsaw, illustrate an adherence to ideas of same-sex relationships being a threat to civilization.[11] By opening *Houses* with a genderless narrator, and including the gender transgressive characters of Kummernis, Paschalis, and Agni and Agni, Tokarczuk problematizes the foundations of such notions.

Another important area of maintaining national identity is the regulation of national minorities. Nationalist discourse relies on an illusion of homogeneity within the nation. The very existence of national minorities, however, subverts any idea of a homogeneous society. In Poland this is well illustrated by the government's fight against bestowing national minority status on the Union of People of Silesian Nationality (ZLNS). To recognize Silesian "nationality" or "ethnicity" would mean admitting that Poland is more than Polish.[12] The character of Peter Dieter, however, a Silesian-German-Pole who lives and dies between borders, is evidence of the impossibility of such homogeneity. The idea of bounded nations also comes into question by setting the novel in such a contested, palimpsestic region as Silesia, where unbounded beings such as Agni are able to come into existence.

CONCLUSION

What ultimately ties together *E. E.*, *Longago and Other Times*, and *House of Day House of Night* is the theme of fluid identities in the context of both political geography and gender. Even before the mass emigrations and immigrations out of and into Silesia after the Second World War, Wrocław, or Breslau, was a border region, home to a "border culture," balancing between the Germanic and Slavic worlds. In her work *Borderlands*, Gloria Anzaldúa describes such a region as "a vague and undetermined place created by the emotional residue of an unnatural boundary. It is in a constant state of transition. The prohibited and forbidden are its inhabitants," and these inhabitants are "those who cross over, pass over, or go through the confines of the 'normal'" (1987, 25). Erna Elztner crosses these confines of the normal through her hybridity, which also makes possible her crossing into and communion with the spirit world. This "border culture" status of Silesia, with Wrocław as its de facto capital, is only heightened in post-war Poland with the arrival of Ukrainian Poles from the eastern Kresy, an "ambiguous" and "marginal" place with no definite borders (Brown, 2004, 2–3). With the forced emigration of Silesian Germans out of and the immigration of Ukrainian Poles of the Kresy into western Poland, this "no-placeness" also moved from east to west. Within this new no-place of Silesia, unity and stability become impossible. In Tokarczuk's universe of *Longago and other Times* and *House of Day House of Night*, this instability of national borders subverts logical reality, replacing it with a *magical* reality in which bodies and nations are unbounded and identities have little meaning. In *Longago* the narrator states that people are "a process," who "are afraid of what is unstable and always changing. They thought up something that does not exist, permanence, decreeing that what is eternal and permanent is perfect" (82). It is an insightful prognosis of the human condition. As processes, we are always in a state of "becoming" rather than "being," or as existential philosophy puts it, our existence precedes our essence. We are not thrown into the world with fully defined identities, and indeed our identities are never not in a process of change and flux. Nationalism, however, cannot admit this kind of flux. It demands "permanence" and the coherence of borders. The maintenance of these borders is only possible through the repression and disregard of national, ethnic, and sexual minorities. This same discourse is born out of the need of patriarchy to maintain exclusive control over the definitions of culture. Tokarczuk's novels work to resist these patriarchal, nationalist regimes, revealing identities as unstable, arbitrary constructions.

NOTES

1. A shorter version of this chapter was published as a chapter as "Transgressions: Palimpsest and the Destruction of Gender and National Borders in Olga Tokarczuk's Dom dzienny, dom nocny," in *The Effect of Palimpsest*, ed. Bożena Shallcross (Frankfurt: Peter Lang, 2011), pp. 195–207.

2. I would like to thank Professor Gary Holcomb for his help with this chapter, which began as a seminar paper for his class on Critical and Literary Theory at Emporia State University.

3. For more on the discussion of the "Recovered Territories" as a propaganda term see Yoshioka (2007).

4. See my discussion in the Introduction on Judith Butler's thoughts on the threat "unregulated permeability" constitutes for hegemonic orders.

5. All English translations from *Longago* come from Tokarczuk, Olga. 2004.

6. Emphasis has been added.

7. For the subject to have been feminine, the subjunctive would need to have been "jakbym była."

8. I borrow the term "palimpsest of sexual identity" here from Mary Galvin's (1999) chapter on H.D. in her work *Queer Poetics: Five Modernist Women Writers*. Galvin uses the idea of palimpsest to forward a political reading of H.D.'s life and work. "Just as contemporary queer poets, historians, theorists, and activists are engaged in excavating the evidence of our continued existence, H.D. was similarly engaged, sifting through the fragments, reclaiming the adulterated stories, writing queers back into the record" (110). This is a superb use of Gérard Genette's ideas on the palimpsest, and one that can be quite helpful in queer readings of other cultural products.

9. Butler's theory of drag seems to fit particularly well in an analysis of the novel, taking into consideration Tokarczuk's own words in an interview with Stanisław Bereś, saying "*Houses* is a novel about transvestites" (*Domy* są powieścią o transwetytach), in Bereś (2002, 503).

10. See my discussion of the Kresy in chapter 2.

11. There have now been a number of gay rights parades officially held in Poland, the first legal one of which I was able to attend in Warsaw in 2006.

12. For more on the recognition of Silesian nationality see Jeziński (2004).

Conclusion

Despite the many totalizing ideologies that vied for control of Poland during the course of the twentieth century, there exist several cultural products that subverted those efforts. Fascists, Soviets, neo-liberals, and the Catholic church all wished to define Poland and Polishness in their own strict terms. The authors whose works I analyze in the previous chapters are just a few of the artists and thinkers who opposed the tyranny of these dogmas. Unfortunately, due to the recent rise of nationalism around the world, renewing efforts to once again set repressive limits on human identification, a project such as this, though focused on the twentieth century, remains depressingly relevant today.

How is a study of literature supposed to help in this struggle? In performing little more than a close reading of texts, can it make an actual impact? By reading the texts transgressively, these explications reveal the slippage and play that exists within constructs conservative ideologies wish to present as solid and fixed. Investigating the convergence between national and gender identities, particularly in works that refuse to conform to traditional nationalist and heteronormative notions of subjectivity, subverts the Catholic-centric nationalism that remains active in Poland—an ideology that continues to enjoy enormous influence in the creation of laws and the formation of norms and morality, especially under the rule of the PiS government.

Homosexual panic—as defined by Eve Sedgwick—is necessarily a nationalist panic, created by the threat of subjects crossing the line between the homosocial and the homoerotic. *TransAtlantyk* and *The Teacher* illustrate the consequences of such a transgression: these disciplinary systems demand a thanatic response. In *TransAtlantyk* when the old Polish father hears about a queer man's erotic desires for his son, his immediate response is to defend his son's honor by trying to kill the "*puto*." Later when it seems that the plan is close to realization, the father's only recourse is to murder his own son rather than see him polluted. For the nation, once the male body has been opened it will be of no further use. In the end, Gombrowicz leaves it a mystery as to whether any murder eventually occurs, refusing to adhere to traditional notions of narrative finality, once again subverting tradition. A similar impulse toward punishment in *The Teacher*, however, ends definitively in tragedy. Although the teacher proves himself to be a patriot and lover of Polish culture, that he would engage in the transgressive act of homoerotic love diminishes him in the eyes of the nationalist regime. He is dismissed from his post due to the father's panic that he will contaminate his sons, making them useless as men. After the oldest son learns of his mentor's indiscretions, he hangs himself out of the same panic, fearing that because of his intimacy with the teacher, though doubtfully physical, he has also been diminished. Patria and nationalism are revealed to be a cult of death in constant struggle against the Philistrian cult of life.

For Polish nationalism to maintain hegemony it must preserve a unitary, homogenous mode of identity formation. The existence of heterogeneous identities undermines nationalist regimes in their attempts to determine who may and may not take part in the nation. The life and work of Julian Stryjkowski challenge this nationalist fantasy of homogeneity. While various nationalist elements saw him simultaneously as either not Polish enough or not Jewish enough, Stryjkowski rejected such binary logic. This struggle with his Polish Jewish identity was complicated further by his queer sexuality during communist rule in Poland, when being outed as gay would very likely have resulted in him losing at the least his livelihood. Despite this, he remained a believer in communism for the rest of his life, even after he left the Party. He illustrated these conflicting characteristics in much of his fiction. *In the Willows* is both a celebration of his Jewish heritage as well as a refusal to leave behind his Polish and communist identities. In *Tommaso del Cavaliere*, Stryjkowski focuses on homoerotic desire rather than his Polish Jewishness. Though it describes events 500 years before his own time, his choice of a first-person, nameless narrator acts to place Stryjkowski within the narrative without directly implicating himself. *Silence* weaves together the difficulties he faced with his Polish Jewish identity and those he faced being a gay man. Though it is his coming-out novel, his reluctance to explicitly describe the narrator's sexual encounters with men reveal the persistent struggle with being gay in both the socialist People's Polish Republic, as well as a more nationalist post-communist Poland.

Marian Pankowski's prose is one of the clearest examples of politically resistant literature in the Polish canon. Along with strong homophobic and xenophobic tendencies, much of modern Polish nationalism is based on an ideology of martyr worship that can be traced back to the messianism of Polish Romantic literature. In his works, especially *Rudolf,* Pankowski anoints himself as the anti-Romantic. The character of Rudolf refuses to admire those who sacrifice themselves for the nation—an act he sees as wasteful and ridiculous. Pankowski's use of unabashed queer erotics subverts traditional Polish values that he viewed as anachronistic and ultimately detrimental to Polish culture due to their masochism and stagnant nature. Instead of venerating moderation and an ethic of self-denial, Rudolf calls for excess and an ethic of *jouissance*, a refusal of the destructive drive inherent in heteronormative regimes.

If nationalism relies on the strict maintenance of sound borders, then any fluidity between those borders is absolutely deadly to the nationalist imaginary. Olga Tokarczuk uses the hybridity of Silesia to illustrate the impossibility of stable borders. Her character Erna Eltzner, being the child of a German father and Polish mother, is the very embodiment of this instability. Through her hybridity she is granted a power denied to the patriarchy, whose authority must remain unquestioned if the nationalist project is to succeed. In the magical area of Longago, borders are mere fantasies that are created in an attempt to better understand the universe. Despite the ease of their transgression, the fantasy of their permanence is vehemently maintained. As a more experimental text, *House of Day House of Night* progresses Tokarczuk's transgressive play with borders much further. Silesia becomes a place where fixed identity of any kind becomes impossible, whether demonstrated in the almost magical transformation of characters' sex, or in the mundane transgression of moving a body from one side of a political border to another. In these descriptions of unstable borders Tokarczuk exposes national and gender identities as arbitrary constructions.

The preceding has been a modest attempt to interfere in the cultural life of Poland. This work is unapologetically political. Literature does not exist outside society, but resides in its very heart. As such, any reading of it is unavoidably influenced by politics. Throughout history, Poland has often found itself as the crossroads between East and West, being pulled at from all sides. It has been the border between competing cultures and ideologies more times than it would have liked. This position, however, does not necessarily have to be one of weakness. If the reality of heterogeneity can be accepted over the fantasy of homogeneity, the hybrid over the pure, the dislocated over the unified, a culture can realize a true strength. In her poem "To live the Borderlands means you," Gloria Anzaldúa gives sound advice for the Polish nation going into the twenty-first century: "To survive the Borderlands / you must live *sin fronteras* / be a crossroads" (1987, 217).

Epilogue

Queer Liberation in the Twenty-First Century, and Jerzy Nasierowski

THE TWENTY-FIRST CENTURY

Queer liberation in Poland in the first two decades of the twenty-first century has experienced several ups and downs. There has undoubtedly been much political progress. In the introduction I mentioned two political figures who, even in the face of Poland's homophobia, have achieved positions in the government. The first is Anna Grodzka, Poland's first openly transgender person in Parliament, and only the third in a national governing body in the world. The second is Robert Biedroń who became both Poland's first openly gay Member of Parliament, and later Poland's first openly gay mayor when he won the mayoral election of Słupsk. What is more, gay rights marches and demonstrations have become a much more common occurrence, and very rarely are they denied permits. In June of 2019, Warsaw was the site of the largest Pride march in Central and Eastern Europe. Unfortunately, the realm of politics in Poland is not very dissimilar to the rest of the world. As has been the case in countries from the United States to Britain to Turkey and India, nationalism has also been on the rise in recent years in Poland. In July of this year, as people began marching in Białystok's first ever Pride Parade, the participants were insulted, threatened, and even physically assaulted by right-wing thugs (John 2019). The city government had given parade permits to thirty-two groups, most of which were in opposition to the Pride parade, despite the recurring acts of violence committed by nationalist gangs. Giving them permits to march on the same day as the Pride parade highlights the government's conviction that it is the quest for tolerance that is transgressive in Polish society, not the willingness to attack peaceful demonstrators.

Happily, in spite of the difficulties posed by politics, the domain of cultural production has also been active in opposing homophobia and nationalism. I discussed several academic works in the introduction, but there have also been contributions to queer literature that are worth noting. One of the most celebrated and infamous Polish authors of the twenty-first century is Michał Witkowski. His 2005 *Lovetown* (Lubiewo) was met with both scandal and praise. It is a brazenly frank novel about the narrator's interviews with older "*cioty*" ("queens," literally "aunties") and their trysts with Soviet soldiers during the PRL that include explicit descriptions of gay sex. Adding to the transgressive value of *Lovetown* is the fact that there is more than one version of the text. Witkowski has repeatedly edited and re-published the novel, creating a work that defies final interpretation. In 2008, Dominika Buczak and Mike Urbaniak published their book *Gaydar* (Gejdar). The text is made up of sixteen interviews the two conducted with gay Poles from every walk of life, ranging in age from eighteen to seventy-five. They discuss a wide range of issues concerning living as a gay person in Poland. Their conversations reveal the heterogeneity of such experience, especially illustrated by their varied political stances.

One of the most prolific contributors to queer and anti-nationalist literature is Korporacja Ha!art publishers. They have republished several of Pankowski's books, including *Rudolf* after being out of print for decades, and also republished Jerzy Nasierowski's uncensored *Crime and . . .* They also published Witkowski's *Lovetown*—at least two of the versions—the aforementioned *Gaydar*, and the Polish translation of Judith Butler's *Gender Trouble* (Uwikłani w płeć). They are at the forefront of publishing new authors who have difficulty getting their work picked up by the older, more established presses. One of their most recent publications, *We're Coming out of the Closet* (2018) by Dr. Jerzy Krzyszpień—which was almost immediately translated into English—discusses the motivations and goals of people who decide to come out as gay or transgender, as well as strategies other people can use in their own coming-out stories.

AN OVERSIGHT

A project on the transgressive in Polish literature is incomplete without mention of Jerzy Nasierowski, an author, actor, and activist once dubbed "first Faggot of the Third Republic." Unfortunately, the sheer volume of his contributions to Polish queer culture, coupled with the difficulty of sufficiently researching him abroad, made it difficult to add a chapter in this book that would do justice to him. I hope, in the future, to write a monograph devoted solely to his work. For now, these few pages must suffice.

Beginning with his two-volume *Zbrodnia i...* (Crime and...), written in the 1980s while he was in prison for aiding and abetting in murder, Nasierowski was an early pioneer of the Queer confessional genre in Poland. His openness in discussing homoerotic desire would not be seen again until Julian Stryjkowski's 1998 *Silence* (Milczenie). Contemporary queer authors owe much to Nasierowski's groundbreaking writing. The transgressive character of his *Ty* (You) trilogy (1992, 1993a, 1993b) of the 1990s acts as a positive force in destabilizing heteronormativity and nationalism. Little has been written about him in Poland aside from news articles. To date none of his work has been translated into English, and if one searches for his name in the MLA International Bibliography there are no results to be found.

Nasierowski was born in 1933. He became an actor and starred in a number of films between 1959 and 1969, growing really quite popular in Poland. There are even stories of teenage girls running after him down the streets of Warsaw. He was handsome, and often played bad-boy roles, so he gained a level of celebrity. This continued until he was arrested in 1973 for aiding and abetting in murder. The crime was committed by his younger boyfriend, but despite his noninvolvement and his cooperation with law enforcement—in fact, Nasierowski informed the police about the actual culprits after two other men were charged—he was convicted and given a life sentence of twenty-five years in prison.

Several sources call his case the most widely publicized (they use the term *"najgłosniejszy"* or *"loudest"*) trial in 1970s Poland (Tomasik 2012, 58). This for me is a rather surprising claim when one considers the political show trials that were abundant throughout the Polish communist period. The infamy of the trial is largely due to the revelation of Nasierowski's sexuality, which was as much on trial as the murder. After the intervention of lawyer Roman Bratny he was released after serving over ten years of his sentence. More than one source has criticized his prosecution as a "show trial," pointing out the Polish government's heavy-handedness against Nasierowski for little other reason than the fact that he was gay. Their punishment of Nasierowski reveals the PRL's panic in the face of homoerotic desire, which many in the Soviet bloc had deemed a "bourgeois deviance."

Years later the PRL's drive to equate the gay with the criminal would be illustrated by the actions of Operation Hyacinth. After the end of Martial Law in 1983 informal gay groups became active. When these groups began receiving help from gay organizations in Vienna, the police began secretly collecting data on them. These activities came to a head in 1985 with Operation Hyacinth. This was a widespread operation around the whole of Poland. The police raided clubs and homes, and rounded up hundreds of gay people for the purposes of fingerprinting and interrogation.[1]

In 1981, while still in prison, Nasierowski published *Jasnozielono-ciemno* (Bright-green Darkness) under the pen-name Jerzy Trębicki, which is one of the few works of communist era Polish literature that openly discusses homoerotic desire in detail. It garnered some notice, but it was overshadowed by the success of his next novel, *Crime and* . . . He wrote this epic eight-hundred-page novel also while in prison, and in 1988 a heavily censored version was published, the first run selling out almost immediately. Like *Bright-green Darkness* he again published under the name Jerzy Trębicki. It is an open, unashamed discussion of prison life, especially of the sexual relationships between prisoners—again a topic that scandalized Polish society.

From 1992 to 1993 he published his *Ty*, or *You* trilogy: *Nasierowski, ty pedale, ty Żydzie!* (Naiserowski, You Fag, You Jew), *Nasierowski, ty antychryście* (Naiserowski, You Antichrist), and *Nasierowski, ty* . . . (Nasierowski, You . . .). For me these are the epitome of post-modern transgressivity. This begins with their material character. They are printed on low quality, pulpy paper, material on which one would expect to read "low" pop fiction or pornography. They also mix genres. The first book is a kind of fictitious memoir, relating the narrator's discovery of several pornographic illustrations that he finds in the cabinet of his venereologist uncle who had recently passed away. These illustrations, which are reminiscent of the works of Aubrey Beardsley and Franz von Bayros, are then reprinted in the text itself. The second book is a mix of short stories, poetry, and even an interview between himself and his alter ego, the pen-name Jerzy Trębicki. The final book is a collection of feuilletons he had previously written for magazines. All three are highly reflexive, often referring to the writing of the text at hand. Their transgressivity is also illustrated in the unabashed, open discussions of homoeroticism, and non-normative sexual activity.

The first book from the series *You Fag, You Jew* opens with the following preface:

> Before prison/the crime, for years I meticulously pretended to be normal. For the sake of my acting career. Unfortunately, whenever the word "homosexual" was mentioned in my company I turned red. After prison, thanks to my book "*Crime and* . . ." I reluctantly assumed the title of "First Faggot of the Third Republic." Unfortunately, our mass media is supposed to make a lot of noise about perverts. So, this phenomenon took on a tribal, pious odor, the even bloody aggression of the Polish nation was replaced by an indifference to us faggots. And along the way, to all sorts of "others . . ." (1992, 9)

Nasierowski's imprisonment is a catalyzing moment. There is a before, when he feels he must hide his sexuality, a time when he is willing to shoulder a quiet shame for it. Then there is an after, when he takes on the mantle of "First Faggot," and refuses to ever be silent again. This trilogy will bear witness to his resolve, being the first of his works to be originally published under his real name.

The title of "First Faggot of the Third Republic" was originally bestowed upon Nasierowski by Jerzy Urban, the infamous founder and editor-in-chief of the satirical leftist weekly tabloid *Nie!* (No!). Truly, Urban's statement was an expression of endearment. His magazine is highly critical of the Polish right wing, especially of the influence of the Catholic Church. It is rather similar to Charlie Hebdo, though not as famous. So, his calling Nasierowski "first faggot" is a similar designation to "first lady," or "first family" of a country. Though he was at first reluctant to assume the title, eventually Nasierowski came to wield it proudly.

The second book of the trilogy, *You Antichrist* . . . , begins with the following manifesto-like preface:

> Every "normal" novel seems to me to be a living corpse that is brazenly dragging itself into the twenty-first century. . . . But perhaps by then there will only be such books in Poland. And of course, their ardent readers as well. . . . I feel so. For now, let every Pole with a sense of humor collect as much of the "abnormal" for that black day as they can. Whether literary, sexual, political, or even ethical. For the moment, mad swordsmen are paralyzing our entire poor nation with so-called Christian values. Otherwise they are very clear-headed careerists.
>
> Residents of every Polish city and village—with a sense of humor—unite! This *Nasierowski, you Antichrist* proposes your participation in super "abnormal" fun (details to follow in this book). (1993a, 9)

Nasierowski achieves a classic deconstruction of normative values. The so-called "normal" comes to represent death, madness, and hypocrisy. The "abnormal" on the other hand is the only force that can lighten the dark day when the normal has taken over the world. It is those who are abnormal that have a sense of humor, through which Poland might be saved. Having a sense of humor becomes something revolutionary, harkening to Marx's call to the workers of the world. It is similar to *Rudolf*'s call to joy, a privileging of *jouissance* over traditional Polish morality.[2] Later he even directly criticizes the Catholic Church and the Polish Pope, John Paul II, for leading the Polish people into the "baleful darkness of the Middle Ages" (9).

The final book, *You* . . . , is a collection of previously published feuilletons, one of which deserves special attention in light of the current political and social climate in Poland. The final piece is entitled "Kaczyński's Husband." The feuilleton was originally published in 1993 in Urban's *No!*. It comes out of a ludicrous spat between then President Lech Wałęsa and then opposition leader and former head of the presidential chancellery, Jarosław Kaczyński, current leader of the ruling conservative Law and Justice party. Wałęsa had implied that Kaczyński was gay. This led to a loud public war of words between the two. Nasierowski used this as fodder for the "onion-like" satirical piece "Kaczyński's Husband," recounting having visited with Pawel Rabiej, Kaczyński's supposed lover. Because of this, Kaczyński sued Wałęsa, Urban, and Nasierowski, who the *Warsaw Voice* described simply as "a sensationalist writer and homosexual with a criminal record." The essay is a criticism of both Wałęsa and Kaczyński. When Wałęsa uses "homosexual" as an insult it is rather reminiscent of the far too common custom in Poland of calling a political enemy a "Jew," implying that the person is untrustworthy, and ultimately anti-Polish. In quoting Kaczyński's own words from *Gazeta Wyborcza* he reveals the deeply imbedded homophobia central to conservative Polish ideology.

Nasierowski has continued to write, and to antagonize conservative Polish culture. In yet another utterly post-modern move he wrote a novel in serial form on gaylife.pl called *That Queer/Faggoty PRL According to Nasierowski*. He is also very active on social media and the Internet, hosting a YouTube channel on which he publishes videos, the topics of which range from the hilarious camp to the serious activist. In all of his work he transgresses normative boundaries, his prose acting as a radical, political criticism of first the PRL and then later of post-socialist, bourgeois Polish society. His frank and unapologetic discussions of homoeroticism challenge the notion of a homogenous, monolithic Polish identity.

NOTES

1. For an in-depth history and analysis of Operation Hyacinth see Szulc (2018, pp. 106–110).
2. See chapter 3.

Bibliography

Adamczyk-Garbowska, Monika. 1998. "Obituary of Julian Stryjkowski 27 April 1905 (Stryj)-8 August 1996 (Warsaw)." In *Focusing on Aspects and Experiences of Religion*, edited by Antony Polonsky, 381–384. London: Littman Library of Jewish Civilization.
———. 2008. "Fiddles on Willow Trees: The Missing Polish Link in the Jewish Canon." In *Arguing the Modern Jewish Canon: Essays on Literature and Culture in Honor of Ruth R. Wisse,* edited by Justin Cammy, Dara Horn, Alyssa Quint, and Rachel Rubinstein, 627–643. Cambridge, MA: Harvard University Press.
Adamowski, Jarosław. 2011. "Marian Pankowski obituary." *The Guardian*, May 18. Accessed April 1, 2019. https://www.theguardian.com/books/2011/may/18/marian-pankowski-obituary.
Anderson, Benedict. 1983. *Imagined Communities: Reflections on the Origin and Spread of Nationalism*. New York: Verso.
Andrzejewski, Jerzy. 1937. Review of *Mill on the River Utrata. Prosto z mostu* 3 (7): 4.
Anzaldúa, Gloria. 1987. *Borderlands: The New Mestiza/La Frontera*. San Francisco: Spinsters/ Aunt Lute.
Augustine, and E. B. Pusey. 1975. *Confessions*. London: Dent.
Baer, Monika. 2009. "'Let Them Hear Us!' The Politics of Same-sex Transgression in Contemporary Poland." In *Transgressive Sex: Subversion and Control in Erotic Encounters*, edited by Hastings Donnan and Fiona Magowan. 131–150. New York: Berghahn Books.
Barbour, Stephen, and Cathie Carmichael. 2000. *Language and Nationalism in Europe*. Oxford: Oxford University Press.
Basiuk, Tomasz, Dominika Ferens, and Tomasz Sikora. 2002. *Odmiany Odmieńca: Mniejszościowe Orientacje Seksualne W Perspektywie Gender = a Queer Mixture: Gender Perspectives on Minority Sexual Identities*. Katowice: Śląsk.
———. 2006a. *Out Here: Local and International Perspectives in Queer Studies*. Newcastle: Cambridge Scholars Press.
———. 2006b. *Parametry Pożądania: Kultura Odmieńców Wobec Homofobii*. Kraków: Universitas.
Beilin, Katarzyna Olga. 2001. "Photographing Sky: Time and Beyond in Tokarczuk and Szymborska." *Polish Review* 46 (4): 441–460.
Bełza, Władysław. 1900. "Katechizm polskiego dziecka." Accessed April 4, 2019. https://wolnelektury.pl/katalog/lektura/katechizm-polskiego-dziecka-katechizm-polskiego-dziecka.html.
Bereś, Stanisław. 2002. *Historia Literatury Polskiej W Rozmowach: Xx-xxi Wiek*. Warsaw: Wydawn. W.A.B.

Berlant, Lauren, and Elizabeth Freeman. 1993. "Queer Nationality." *Fear of a Queer Planet: Queer Politics and Social Theory*, edited by Michael Warner. Minneapolis: University of Minnesota Press, 193–229.

Bhabha, Homi K. 1994. *The Location of Culture*. London: Routledge.

Bikont, Anna, and Joanna Szczęsna. 2006. "Moją Ojczyzną Jest Język." *Gazeta Wyborcza*, August 13.

Borkowska, Grażyna. 2002. "The Homelessness of the Other: The Homoerotic Experience in the Prose of Julian Stryjkowski." In *Framing the Polish Home: Postwar Cultural Constructions of Hearth, Nation, and Self*, edited by Bożena Shallcross, 54–67. Athens, OH: Ohio State University Press.

Branach-Kallas, Anna, and Katarzyna Więckowska, eds. 2004. Introduction to *The Nation of the Other: Constructions of Nation in Contemporary Cultural and Literary Discourses*. 7–10. Toruń, Poland: Wydawnictwo Uniwersytetu Mikołaja Kopernika.

Brown, Kate. 2004. *A Biography of No Place: From Ethnic Borderland to Soviet Heartland*. Cambridge, MA: Harvard University Press.

Buczak, Dominika and Mike Urbaniak. 2008. *Gejdar*. Kraków: Korporacja Ha!art.

Bugajski, Leszek. 1993. "Co oznacza *Milczenie*?" *Twórczość* 11: 112–114.

Butler, Judith. 1990. *Gender Trouble: Feminism and the Subversion of Identity*. New York: Routledge.

———. 1991. "Imitation and Gender Subordination." *In Inside/out: Lesbian Theories, Gay Theories*, edited by Diana Fuss and Michèle Aina Barale, 13–31. New York: Routledge.

Bynum, Caroline W. 1987. *Holy Feast and Holy Fast: The Religious Significance of Food to Medieval Women*. Berkeley: University of California Press.

Chowaniec, Urszula. 2010. "'Intimately Social': The Experience of Menstruation in Polish Women's Writing." In *Mapping Experience in Polish and Russian Women's Writing*, edited by Marja Rytkönen, 150–170. Newcastle upon Tyne: Cambridge Scholars,

Chudoba, Ewa. 2012. *Literatura i homoseksualność: Zarys problematyki genderowej w kanonicznych tekstach literatury światowej i Polskiej*. Kraków: Wydawnictwo Libron.

Cixous, Helene. 1976. "Laugh of the Medusa." *Signs* 1 (4): 875–893.

Czabanowska-Wróbel Anna. 1995. "Kształt miłości niemożliwej: O Milczeniu Juliana Stryjkowskiego." Teksty drugie 32 (2): 163–170.

Czermińska, Małgorzata. 2019. *The Autobiographical Triangle: Witness, Confession, Challenge*. Translated by Jean Ward. Berlin: Peter Lang.

De Bruyn, Dieter, Kris Van Heuckelom, and Dorota Walczak. 2011. "Here Comes Pankowski: Adventures in Ambiguity." *Russian, Croatian And Serbian, Czech And Slovak, Polish Literature* 70 (4): 467–478.

Donnan, Hastings, and Fiona Magowan. 2009. "Sexual Transgression, Social Order and the Self." In *Transgressive Sex: Subversion and Control in Erotic Encounters*, edited by Hastings Donnan and Fiona Magowan. 1–24. New York: Berghahn Books.

Doubrovsky, Serge. 1977. *Fils*. Paris: Galilee.

Foucault, Michel. 1977. "A Preface to Transgression." In *Language, Counter-Memory, Practice: Selected Essays and Interviews*, edited and translated by Donald F. Bouchard, and Sherry Simon. 29–52. Ithaca, NY: Cornell University Press.

———. 1995. *Discipline and Punish: The Birth of the Prison*. Translated by Alan Sheridan. New York: Random House.

Fuss, Diana. 1991. Introduction to *Inside/out: Lesbian Theories, Gay Theories*. New York: Routledge. 1–10.

Galvin, Mary E. 1999. *Queer Poetics: Five Modernist Women Writers*. London: Praeger.

Gasyna, George Z. 2011. *Polish, Hybrid, and Otherwise: Exilic Discourse in Joseph Conrad and Witold Gombrowicz*. New York: Continuum.

Gorczyńska, Renata. 1988. "Furia Słów Mariana Pankowskiego." *Kultura: Szkice, Opowiadania, Sprawozdania* 7: 158–163.

Gombrowicz, Witold. 1937. *Ferdydurke*. Paris: Instytut Literacki.

———. 1977. *Testament: Entretiens de DOminique de Roux avec Gombrowicz*. Paris: P. Belfond.

———. 1988. *Diary Volume 1*. Translated by Lillian Vallee. Evanston: Northwestern University Press.
———. 1994. *TransAtlantyk*. Translated by Carolyn French and Nina Karsov. New Haven: Yale University Press.
———. 2000. *Ferdydurke*. Translated by Danuta Borchardt. New Haven: Yale University Press.
Gopinath, Gayatri. 2005. *Impossible Desires: Queer Diasporas and South Asian Public Cultures*. Durham: Duke University Press.
Gorczyńska, Renata. 1988. "Furia Słów Mariana Pankowskiego." *Kultura: Szkice, Opowiadania, Sprawozdania* 7 (8): 158–63.
Gough, Val. 2000. "The lesbian Christ: Body Politics in Hélène Cixous's *Le livre de Promethea*." In *Body Matters: Feminism, Textuality, Corporeality*, edited by Angela Keane and Avril Horner. 234–243. Manchester: Manchester University Press, 2000.
Grimstad, Knut A, and Ursula Phillips. 2005. Introduction to *Gender and Sexuality in Ethical Context: Ten Essays on Polish Prose*. 7–17. Bergen: Department of Russian Studies, University of Bergen.
Gronczewski, Andrezej. 1972. *Jarosław Iwaszkiewicz*. Paŕstwowy Instytut Wydawniczy.
Iwasiów, Inga. 2011. "Whither from the Motherland? Some Comments on Female Characters in Marian Pankowski's Writings." *Russian, Croatian And Serbian, Czech And Slovak, Polish Literature* 70 (4): 479–495.
Iwaszkiewicz, Jarosław. 1933. *Brzezina*. Warsaw: Gebethner i Wolff.
———. 1936. *Młyn nad Utratą*. Warsaw: Gebethner i Wolff.
———. 1956. *Sława i chwała*. Warsaw: PIW.
———. 1966. *Nauczyciel*. In *Opowiadania Wybrane*. 185–248. Warsaw: Czytelnik.
———. 1969. *Opowiadania wybrane*. Warsaw: Czytelnik.
Jackson, Robert Louis. 2007. "Chekhov's 'Rothschild's Fiddle': 'By the Rivers of Babylon' in Easter Orthodox Liturgy." In *Chekhov the Immigrant: Translating a Cultural Icon*, edited by Michael C. Finke, Sherbinin J. W. De, and Robert Coles. 201–206. Bloomington, IN: Slavica.
Jeziński, Marek. 2004. "Excluding the Other: The Concept of Nation in Contemporary Political Discourse in Poland." In *The Nation of the Other: Constructions of Nation in Contemporary Cultural and Literary Discourses*, edited by Anna Branach-Kallas and Katarzyna Więckowska, 25–36. Toruń, Poland: Wydawnictwo Uniwersytetu Mikołaja Kopernika.
Jöhling, Wolfgang and Julian Stryjkowski. 1992. *Dyskretne Namiętności: Antologia Polskiej Prozy Homoerotycznej*. Poznań: Softpress.
John, Tara. 2019. "A city's first pride march was meant to be a day of joy. The far right turned it into chaos." *CNN.com* July 28. Accessed August 1, 2019. https://www.cnn.com/2019/07/28/europe/bialystok-pride-lgbtq-far-right-intl/index.html.
Kaliściak, Tomasz. 2016. *Płeć pantofla: Odmieńcze męskości w polskiej prozie XIX i XX wieku*. Olsztyn, Poland: Instytut Badań Literackich PAN.
Karpiuk, Dawid. 2019. "Premier Gliński ubolewa. A ja razem z nim." *Newsweek Poland*, August 8. Accessed August 18, 2019. https://www.newsweek.pl/opinie/premier-glinski-ubolewa-a-ja-razem-z-nim/zm6wx8t.
Kasztelan, Marta, Marta Soszynska, and Agnieszka Liggett. 2015. "Pretty Radical: A Young Woman's Journey into the Heart of Poland's Far Right." TheGuardian.com video, 16:31. https://www.theguardian.com/world/video/2015/jan/19/pretty-radical-young-woman-poland-far-right-video.
Kołakowski, Leszek. 2002. Introduction to *The Birch Grove and Other Stories, by Jarosław Iwaszkiewicz*, translated by Antonia Lloyd-Jones, vii-xvi. Budapest: Central European University Press.
Konopnicka, Maria. 1907. "Rota." In Maria Szypowska, ed. 1963. *Konopnicka jakiej nie znamy*, Warsaw: Panstwowy Instytut Wydawniczy, 32.
Kot, Wiesław. 1997. *Julian Stryjkowski*. Poznań: Dom Wydawniczy Rebis.
Kozlowska, Hanna. 2013. "Rainbow Becomes a Prism to View Gay Rights." *New York Times* March 31. Accessed April 4, 2019. https://www.nytimes.com/2013/03/22/world/europe/in-warsaw-rainbow-sculpture-draws-attacks.html.

Krupiński, Piotr. 2011. "About the Revolutions of 'Planet Auschwitz': Marian Pankowski's Lecture on Anti-Martyrological Literature." *Russian, Croatian And Serbian, Czech And Slovak, Polish Literature* 70 (4): 553–571.

Krzyszpień, Jerzy. 2018. *We're Coming out of the Closet*. Kraków: Korporacja Ha!art.

Kucharski, Alan. 1998. "Witold, Witold, and Witold: Performing Gombrowicz." In *Gombrowicz's Grimaces: Modernism, Gender, Nationality*, edited by Ewa Płonowska-Ziarek. 267–286. Albany: State University of New York Press.

Latawiec, Krystyna. 2011. "Marian Pankowski: Between the Carpathians and European Civilization." *Russian, Croatian And Serbian, Czech And Slovak, Polish Literature* 70 (4): 539–551.

Leerssen, Joep. 2006. *National Thought in Europe: A Cultural History*. Amsterdam: Amsterdam University Press.

Lorentowicz, Jan. 1936. Review of *The Mill on the River Utrata* by Jarosław Iwaskziewicz. *Nowa Książka* 3 (10): 582–583.

McDonough, Sarah P. 2011. "How to Read Autofiction." BA thesis, Wesleyan University.

Maher, Bill, Shane Smith, and Eddy Moretti. 2015. "A Prayer for Uganda." Vice News video, 29:02. *HBO.com*.

Marsden, Phillip. 2002. "Poles Apart: Olga Torkarczuk claims her place among the greats of Polish letters with *House of Day, House of Night*." *TheGuardian.com*, October 19. Accessed April 4, 2019. https://www.theguardian.com/books/2002/oct/20/fiction.features2.

Mickiewicz, Adam. 1992. *Pan Tadeusz*. Translated by Kenneth R. Mackenzie. New York: Hippocrene Books.

Mikoś, Michael J. 2002. *Polish Romantic Literature: An Anthology*. Bloomington, IN: Slavica.

Mincer, Laura Quercioli. 2001. "A Voice from the Diaspora: Julian Stryjkowski." *In Studies from POLIN: From Shtetl to Socialism*, edited by Antony Polonsky, 487–501. London: The Littman Library of Jewish Civilization.

Mizielińska, Joanna. 2001. "The Rest is Silence: Polish Nationalism and the Question of Lesbian Existene." *The European Journal of Women's Studies* 8 (3): 281–197.

Mucha, Janusz. 1997. "Getting Out of the Closet: Cultural Minorities in Poland Cope with Oppression." *East European Quarterly* 31 (3): 299–309.

Murav, Harriet. 2011. *Music from a Speeding Train: Jewish Literature in Post-Revolution Russia*. Stanford, CA: Stanford University Press.

Nasierowski, Jerzy. 1981. *Jasnozielonociemno*. Warsaw: Czytelnik.

———. 1992. *Nasierowski, ty pedale, ty Żydzie!* Warsaw: Reporter.

———. 1993a. *Nasierowski, ty antychryście*. Warsaw: Reporter.

———. 1993b. *Nasierowski, ty...* Warsaw: Reporter.

———. 2006. *Zbrodnia i...* Kraków: Korporacja Ha!art.

Niżyńska, Joanna. 2013. *The Kingdom of Insignificance: Miron Białoszewski and the Quotidian, the Queer, and the Traumatic*. Evanston: Northwestern University Press.

Pankowski, Marian. 1983. *Matuga idzie: przygody*. Lublin: Wydawnictwo Lubelskie.

———. 1984. *Rudolf*. Warsaw: Czytelnik.

———. 1993. "Garb." *Dialog: Miesiecznik Poswiecony Dramaturgii Wspolczesnej: Teatralnej, Filmowej, Radiowej, Telewizyjnej* 38 (1): 161–162.

———. 1996. *Rudolf*. Translated by John Maslen, and Elizabeth Maslen. Evanston, IL: Northwestern University Press.

———. 2000. *Z Auszwicu Do Belsen: Przygody*. Warsaw: Czytelnik.

Pankowski, Rafał. 2006. "Poland." In *World Fascism: A Historical Encyclopedia*, edited by Cyprian Blamires. Santa Barbara: ABC-CLIO.

Parker, Andrew, Mary Russo, Doris Sommer, and Patricia Yaeger. 1992. *Nationalisms and Sexualities*. New York: Routledge.

Pasterska, Jolanta. 2011. "Marian Pankowski And Polishness: The Literary Provocations of an Émigré." *Russian, Croatian And Serbian, Czech And Slovak, Polish Literature* 70 (4): 525–537.

Piekarska. Magda. 2015a. "Olga Tokarczuk: To ja jestem patriotką, a nie nacjonalista palący kukłę Żyda." Gazeta Wyborcza, December 10. Accessed April 4, 2019. http://wroclaw.wyborcza.pl/wroclaw/1,142076,19325258,olga-tokarczuk-to-ja-jestem-patriotka-a-nie-nacjonalista-palacy.html.

———. (2015b). "Nowa polityka historyczna wg PiS. Żądają odebrania Tokarczuk obywatelstwa Nowej Rudy." *Gazeta Wyborcza*, December 15. Accessed April 4, 2019. http://wyborcza.pl/1,75410,19347868,nowa-polityka-historyczna-wg-pis-zadaja-odebrania-tokarczuk.html.

Piekarski, Ireneusz. 2010. *Z ciemności: o twórczości Juliana Stryjkowskiego*. Wrocław: Wydawnictwo Uniwersytetu Wrocławskiego.

Plato. *Symposium*. 1994. Translated and with an introduction by Robin Waterfield. Oxford: Oxford University Press.

Płonowska-Ziarek, Ewa. 1998a. Introduction to *Gombrowicz's Grimaces: Modernism, Gender, Nationality*. 1–30. Albany: State University of New York Press.

———. 1998b. "The Scar of the Foreigner and the Fold of the Baroque: National Affiliations and Homosexuality in Gombrowicz's *Trans-Atlantyk*." In *Gombrowicz's Grimaces: Modernism, Gender, Nationality*, edited by Ewa Płonowska-Ziarek, 213–244. Albany: State University of New York Press.

Plucinska, Joanna. 2018. "Gay couple can register child in conservative Poland: court." *Reuters.com*, October 11. Accessed December 5, 2019. https://www.reuters.com/article/us-poland-gayrights/gay-couple-can-register-child-in-conservative-poland-court-idUSKCN1ML1OQ.

"Poland: Gay Pride Starts with a Kiss and Ends with Violence." 2013. Filmed May 18 in Kraków, Poland. YouTube video, 1:13. https://www.youtube.com/watch?v=Aeqp4KOMJ4A.

"Poland Elects its First Openly Gay Mayor." 2015. *The Guardian*, December 1. Accessed April 4, 2019. https://www.theguardian.com/world/2014/dec/01/poland-elects-openly-gay-mayor-robert-biedron.

"Poland Swears in First Transsexual and Gay MPs." 2011. *BBC News*, November 8. Accessed April 4, 2019. https://www.bbc.com/news/world-europe-15630789.

Polonsky, Antony, and Monika Adamczyk-Garbowska, eds. 2001. *Contemporary Jewish Writing in Poland: An Anthology*. Lincoln: University of Nebraska Press.

Prus, Bolesław. 1890. *Lalka*. Warsaw: Gebethner i Wolff.

Przybylski, Ryszard K. 1970. *Eros I Tanatos: Proza Jarosława Iwaszkiewicza, 1916–1938*. Warsaw: Czytelnik.

———. 1993. "Ciemności Mariana Pankowskiego." *Dialog: Miesiecznik Poswiecony Dramaturgii Wspolczesnej: Teatralnej, Filmowej, Radiowej, Telewizyj* 38 (1):163–167.

Puar, Jasbir K. 2017. *Terrorist Assemblages: Homonationalism in Queer Times*. Durham, NC: Duke University Press.

Ritz, German. 1996. *Jarosław Iwaszkiewicz: Ein Grenzgänger Der Moderne*. Bern: Peter Lang.

———. 2002. *Nić w Labiryncie Pożądania: Gender i Płeć w Literaturze Polskiej od Romantyzmu do Postmodernizmu*. Warsaw: Wiedza Powszechna.

———. 2005. "Inexpressible Desire and Narrative Poetics: Homosexuality in Iwaszkiewicz, Breza, Mach and Gombrowicz." In *Gender and Sexuality in Ethical Context: Ten Essays on Polish Prose*, edited by Knut Andreas Grimstad and Ursula Phillips. 254–276. Bergen: Department of Russian Studies, University of Bergen.

Rohoziński, Janusz. 1968. *Jarosław Iwaskiewicz*. Warsaw: Paristwowe Zakłady Wydawn. Szkolnych.

Ruta-Rutkowska, Krystyna. 2008. *Szkice O Twórczości Mariana Pankowskiego*. Warsaw: Wydano Nakł. Wydziału Polonistyki Uniwersytetu Warszawskiego.

"Sad GAY Parade in Kraków." 2015. Filmed May 13 in Kraków, Poland. YouTube video, 3:38. https://www.youtube.com/watch?v=hy5KaddMawc.

Sadowska, Małgorzata. 2001. "Rasa przeklęta: O prozie Juliana Stryjkowskiego." In *Ciało, płeć, literatura: prace ofiarowane profesorowi Germanowi Ritzowi w pięćdziesiątą rocznicę urodzin*, edited by Magdalena Hornung et al., 379–394. Warsaw: Wiedza Powszechna.

Sedgwick, Eve K. 1990. *Epistemology of the Closet*. Berkeley: University of California Press.

Selerowicz, Andrzej. 1993. "Odmieńcy: Jarosław Iwaszkiewicz 1894–1980." *Inaczej: pismo mniejszosci seksualnych* 4 (7): 37.

Sempruch, Justyna. 2008a. *Fantasies of Gender and the Witch in Feminist Theory and Literature*. West Lafayette, IN: Purdue University Press.
———. 2008b. "Patriarchy in Post-1989 Poland and Tokarczuk's *Dom dzienny, dom nocny* (The Day House, the Night House)." *CLCWeb: Comparative Literature and Culture* 10 (3). Accessed April 4, 2019. https://docs.lib.purdue.edu/cgi/viewcontent.cgi?article=1375&context=clcweb. 1–9.
Shallcross, Bożena. 2011. "The Pink Triangle and Gay Camp Identity in Marian Pankowski's Writings." *Russian, Croatian And Serbian, Czech And Slovak, Polish Literature* 70 (4): 511–523.
Shiach, Morag. 1991. *Hélène Cixous: A Politics of Writing*. London: Routledge.
Sikora, Tomasz. 2004. "Queering the Heterosexist Fantasy of the Nation." In *The Nation of the Other: Constructions of Nation in Contemporary Cultural and Literary Discourses*, edited by Anna Branach-Kallas and Katarzyna Więckowska, 65–78. Toruń, Poland: Wydawnictwo Uniwersytetu Mikołaja Kopernika.
Sobolewska, Anna. 2003. *Maski Pana Boga: Szkice O Pisarzach I Mistykach*. Kraków: Wydawn. Literackie.
Śpiewak, Pawel. 1974. "Miedzy Austerią I Ameryką." *Tworczosc* 30 (9): 97–103.
Stallybrass, Peter, and Allon White. 1986. *The Politics and Poetics of Transgression*. Ithaca, NY: Cornell University Press.
Stefańczyk, Iwona. 2004. "O 'słusznej dyskryminacji.'" In *Homofobia po polsku*, edited by Przemysław Pilarski, 175–782. Warsaw: Wydawnictwo Sic!
Stola, Dariusz. 2000. *Kampania antysyjonistyczna w Polsce 1967–1968*. Warsaw: Instytut Studiów Politycznych PAN,.
Stryjkowski, Julian. 1961. "Ajeleth." *Imię własne: Opowiadania*. Warsaw: Czytelnik.
———. 1972a. *The Inn*. Translated by Celina Wieniewska. New York: Harcourt.
———. 1972b. Letter to Mr. and Mrs. Paul Eufel, February 1972, Warsaw, Poland. Records of International Writing Program, collection number RG06.0012.009, Box # 20 [STEL—TART]. Iowa City, IA: IWP Archives, University of Iowa.
———. 1974. *Na Wierzbach . . . Nasze Skrzypce*. Warsaw: Cytelnik.
———. 1982. *Tommaso del Cavaliere*. Warsaw: Państwowy Instytut Wydawniczy.
———. 1993. *Milczenie*. Kraków: Wydawnictwo Literackie.
———. 2001a. "Judas Maccabeus: Afterword." Translated by Christopher Garbowski. In *Contemporary Jewish Writing in Poland: An Anthology*, edited by Antony Polonsky and Monika Adamczyk-Garbowska, 54–56. Lincoln: University of Nebraska Press.
———. 2001b. "Voices in the Darkness: Excerpts." Translated by Christopher Garbowski. In *Contemporary Jewish Writing in Poland: An Anthology*, edited by Antony Polonsky and Monika Adamczyk Garbowska, 5–53. Lincoln: University of Nebraska Press.
Sypniewski, Zbyszek, and Błażej Warkocki, eds. 2004. *Homofobia Po Polsku*. Warsaw: Wydawnictwo Sic!
Szczuka, Kazimiera. 2000. "Spinners, Weavers, and Spiders: Remarks about Women's Creativity." In *Feminist Critique: Sister of Literary Theory and History*, edited by G. Borkowska and Liliana Sikorska, 69–79. Warsaw: IBL.
Szewc, Piotr. 1984. *Wielki strach*. Warsaw: Nowa.
———. 1991. *Ocalony na Wschodzie. Z Julianem Stryjkowskim rozmawia Piotr Szewc*. Montricher: Les Editions Noir sur Blanc.
Szulc, Lukasz. 2018. *Transnational Homosexuals in Communist Poland: Cross-Border Flows in Gay and Lesbian Magazines*. Cham, Switzerland: Palgrave Macmillan.
Termer, Janusz. 2009. *Z przełomu wieków, Czyli litertury dzień powszedni (1990–2008)*. Toruń: Wydawn. Adam Marszałek.
Tokarczuk, Olga. 1995. *E. E.* Warsaw: Państwowy Instytut Wydawniczy.
———. 1996. *Prawiek i inne czasy*. Warsaw: Wydawnictwo W.A.B.
———. 1998. *Dom dzienny, dom nocny*. Walbrzych: Wydawnictwo Ruta.
———. 2000. *Lalka i perła*. Kraków: Wydawnictwo Literackie.
———. 2004. "*Longago and Other Times*: A Novel by Olga Tokarczuk with Introduction." Translated by Jack J. Hutchens. MA thesis, Emporia State University.

———. 2008. Introduction to *Uwikłani w płeć: Feminizm i polityka tożsamości*. 5–10. Warsaw: Wydawnictwo Krytyki Politycznej.
Tomasik, Krzysztof. 2008. *Homobiografie: Pisarki i pisarze polscy XIX i XX wieku*. Warsaw: Wydawnictwo Krytyki Politycznej.
———. 2012. *Gejerel: Mniejszości seksualne w Prl-U*. Warsaw: Wydawnictwo Krytyki Politycznej.
Trochimczyk, Maja. 2000. "Sacred versus Secular: The Convoluted History of Polish Anthems." In *After Chopin: Essays in Polish Music*. Vol. 6 of *Polish Music History Series*, edited by Maja Trochimczyk. Los Angeles: Friends of Polish Music at USC.
Trojanowska, Tamara, Joanna Niżyńska, and Przemysław Czapliński. 2018. *Being Poland: A New History of Polish Literature and Culture since 1918*. Toronto: University of Toronto Press.
Turczyn, Anna. 2007. "Autofikcja, czyli autobiografia psychopolifoniczna." *Teksty drugie*, (1–2) 204–211.
Wajda, Andrzej, dir. 1999. *Pan Tadeusz*. Poland: Pomaton. DVD.
Wampuszyc, Ewa V. 2014. "Magical Realism in Olga Tokarczuk's *Primeval and Other Times* and *House of Day, House of Night*." *East European Politics and Societies and Cultures* 28 (2): 366–385.
Warkocki, Błażej. 2007. *Homo niewiadomo: polska proza wobec odmienności*. Warsaw: Sic!.
———. 2019. "What Really Happened Aboard the Banbury? Reading Gombrowicz with Eve Kosofsky Sedwick." In *Gombrowicz in Transnational Context: Translation, Affect, and Politics*. New York: Routledge. 126–141.
Wilson, Reuel K. 1997. Review of *Rudolf*, by Marian Pankowski, translated by John Maslen, and Elizabeth Maslen. *World Literature Today*. Autumn, 829.
Witkowski, Michał. 2005. *Lubiewo*. Kraków: Korporacja Ha!art.
Wolfreys, Julian. 2008. *Transgression: Identity, Space, Time*. New York: Palgrave MacMillan.
Wiktowski, Michał. 2006. *Lubiewo*. Kraków: Korporacja Ha!art.
Yoshioka, Yun. 2007. "Imagining Their Lands as Ours: Place Name Changes on Ex-German Territories in Poland after World War II." *Slavic Eurasian Studies* 15 (3): 273–287.
Zamoyski, Adam. 2009. *Poland: A History*. New York: Hippocrene.
Zawada, Andrzej. 1994. *Jarosław Iwaszkiewicz*. Warsaw: Wiedza Powszechna.
Zubrzycki, Geneviève. 2006. *The Crosses of Auschwitz: Nationalism and Religion in Post-Communist Poland*. Chicago: The University of Chicago Press.
———. 2007. "The cross, the Madonna, and the Jew: Persistent Symbolic Representations of the Nation in Poland." In *Nationalism in a Global Era: The Persistence of Nations*, edited by Mitchell Young, Eric Zuelow, and Andreas Sturm. 118–139. New York: Routledge.

Index

Adamczyk-Garbowska, Monika, 52, 57, 62, 72
Adamowski, Jarosław, 77, 78
"Ajeleth," 71, 72
Anderson, Benedict, 10, 21n7
Andrzejewski, Jerzy, 26
anti-Semitism, 16, 54, 65
Anzaldúa, Gloria, 101, 118, 123
Augustine, Saint, 55
Austeria. See Inn, The
autofiction, 18, 53, 54, 62, 64, 80

Basiuk, Tomasz, 6
Bełza, Władysław, 15
Berlant, Lauren, 2, 92
Bhabha, Homi K., 10, 55, 72
Biedroń, Robert, 17, 125
Borkowska, Grażyna, 9, 51, 60, 71
Brown, Kate, 50n2, 72, 118
Butler, Judith, 9, 10, 21n5, 25, 97, 104, 111, 113, 119n4, 119n9, 126

"Catechism of the Polish Child," 15–16
Catholicism and the Catholic Church, 1, 8, 14, 15, 16–17, 121, 129
Chowaniec, Urszula, 99–100
Christ of Nations, 13, 39, 47, 50n15, 79, 90
Chudoba, Ewa, 6, 26, 28, 50n8, 53
Cixous, Hélène, 100, 101, 102, 105

communism, 1, 20, 23, 51, 52, 53, 54, 56, 57, 60, 62, 63, 65, 66, 67, 73, 79, 87, 95, 106, 107, 122, 127, 128
compulsory heterosexuality, 6, 9, 10, 25, 48, 60

Dmowski, Roman, 14, 16
Dom dzienny, dom nocny. See House of Day, House of Night
Dyskretne namiętności (Discrete Passions), 1

E.E., 20, 95, 97, 98–105, 109, 118, 127
Epistemology of the Closet, 24, 30
Eros and Thanatos (erotic and thanatic), 20, 23, 26, 29, 30, 32, 34, 36, 42, 48, 81, 85, 87, 121

Fear of a Queer Planet, 2
Ferens, Dominka, 6
Foucault, Michel, 2, 5, 6, 46
Freeman, Elizabeth, 2, 92
Freud, Sigmund and the Freudian, 26, 67, 103
From Auschwitz to Belsen: Adventures, 75, 79, 80, 85
Fuss, Diana, 5–6, 10, 11

Gasyna, George Z., vii, 39, 40
gay pride parades, 3, 4, 125

Gombrowicz, Witold, 6, 16, 18, 20, 23–24, 38–48, 49, 50n1, 50n12–50n14, 50n18, 51, 55, 75, 80, 87, 92, 95, 121
Grimstad, Knut A., 39
Grodzka, Anna, 17, 125

Here Comes Matuga: Adventures, 78, 80, 85, 89
heteronormativity, 2, 4, 7, 8, 12, 20, 21, 24, 25, 26, 34, 36, 42, 43, 43–44, 46, 48, 49, 51, 75, 83, 84, 87, 92, 94, 97, 117, 121, 122, 127
homoeroticism, 1, 4, 26, 38, 60, 61–63, 69, 73, 81, 87, 95, 121, 122, 127, 128, 130
homophobia, 1, 3, 6, 16, 17, 44, 46, 49, 50n3, 50n14, 68, 75, 96, 122, 125, 126, 129
homosexual panic, 20, 23, 24, 25, 26, 37, 42, 46, 48, 50n1, 50n3, 121
homosociality, 24, 25, 36, 37, 43, 48, 66, 121
House of Day, House of Night, 20, 95, 96, 97, 109–117, 118, 119n9, 123

identity and its creation: as oppositional process, 5–6, 10, 11, 45; national, 10; through performance and performativity, 9–10
Imagined Communities, 10
In the Williows . . . Our Fiddles, 8, 20, 51, 53, 58, 62, 73n10
Inn, The, 73n2
Iwaszkiewicz, Jarosław, 20, 23, 26, 30, 36, 37, 48, 49, 50n8, 61, 75, 95

Kaczyński, Jarosław, 129
Kaliściak, Tomasz, 6, 50n18
Kołakowski, Leszek, 23, 52
Konopnicka, Maria, 14, 15, 22n11
Korporacja Ha!art, 126
Kresy, 24, 50n2, 64, 72, 114, 116, 118, 119n10

Law and Justice (PiS), 16, 96, 105, 121, 129
League of Polish Families (LPR), 16, 105
Leerssen, Joep, 10, 11, 43
LGBTQ+ groups, 17

Longago and Other Times, 20, 95, 97, 106–108, 109, 118, 119n5, 123
Lovetown, 126

marsz równości. *See* gay pride parades
Martial Law, 63, 127
Matuga idzie: prygody. See Here Comes Matuga: Adventures
Mickiewicz, Adam, 13, 25, 78
Milczenie. See Silence
Mizielińska, Joanna, 11

Nasierowski, Jerzy, 21, 126, 126–127, 128, 129, 129–130
nationalism, 1, 2, 6, 8, 10, 11, 12, 13–14, 16, 17, 20, 23, 24, 39, 41, 43, 44, 46, 48, 49, 50n16, 64, 64–65, 71, 75, 80, 81, 88, 89–90, 94, 97, 98, 105, 118, 121–123, 125, 126, 127
nationalist Polish groups, 16–17, 125
Nauczyciel. See Teacher, The
Na Wierzbach . . . Nasze Skrzypce. See In the Williows . . . Our Fiddles

Operation Hyacinth, 63, 127, 130n1

Pankowski, Marian, 20, 75–77, 78, 79, 80, 81, 85, 87, 88, 89, 92, 94, 94n4, 94n6, 94n7, 95, 122, 126
"Pan Tadeusz," 25, 35, 39, 44, 48, 50n11, 50n17, 78
partitions, 13, 21, 25, 50n15
PiS. *See* Law and Justice
Plato, 28, 62, 104
"Pledge, The," 14–15
Polak-Katolik, 14, 17
Polish academic works on Queer studies, 6, 8, 9
Polska Rzeczpospolita Ludowa (PRL: Polish People's Republic), 79, 95, 126, 127, 130
Prawiek i inne czasy. See Longago and Other Times
Puar, Jasbir K., 13

Queer Nation, 2

Ritz, German, 26, 30, 49

Romanticism, 13, 14, 20, 23, 25, 39, 41, 42, 44, 47, 50n3, 50n15, 76, 78, 79, 84, 90, 92, 94, 122
"Rota". *See* "Pledge, The"
"Rothschild's Fiddle," 59, 73n10

Sedgwick, Eve K., 20, 23, 24, 25, 26, 30, 42, 48, 50n1, 50n3, 50n10, 61, 121
Sikora, Tomasz, 6, 11, 25, 50n4
Silence, 20, 51, 63–71, 73, 122, 127
Stallybrass, Peter, 2, 5
Stryjkowski, Julian, 20, 51–54, 55, 56, 57, 58, 58–60, 61–63, 64, 65, 66, 69–71, 71, 72–73, 73n1, 73n2, 73n5, 95, 122, 127
Szewc, Piotr, 66, 73

Teacher, The, 20, 23, 24, 26, 26–38, 42, 48, 49, 51, 61, 62, 83, 94n5, 121
Tokarczuk, Olga, 20, 95–97, 97, 99, 100, 105, 106, 109, 110, 114, 115, 117, 118, 119n1, 119n5, 119n9, 123
Tomasik, Krzysztof, 6, 23, 24, 50n6, 127
Tommaso del Cavaliere, 20, 62, 63, 73, 122

TransAtlantyk, 18, 19, 20, 23, 24, 26, 38–48, 48–49, 50n12, 50n13, 51, 55, 80, 92, 94n5, 95, 121
transgression and the transgressive, 1–6, 7–9, 19, 23, 25, 30, 34, 36, 37, 38, 41, 43, 48, 51, 62, 66, 75, 83, 84, 86, 87, 88, 97, 106, 107, 108, 109, 112, 113, 114, 115, 116, 117, 121, 123, 125, 126, 127, 128, 130
Trojanowska, Tamara, 8, 9

"Ubu Roi," 21
Urban, Jerzy, 129

Wałęsa, Lech, 129
Wampuszyc, Ewa V., 97, 106, 108
White, Allon, 2, 5
Witkowski, Michał, 126
Wolfreys, Julian, 5, 7–8

Z Auszwicu Do Belsen: Przygody. *See From Auschwitz to Belsen: Adventures*

About the Author

Jack J. B. Hutchens received his PhD in Polish literature from the Department of Slavic Languages and Literatures at the University of Illinois Urbana-Champaign. He has authored several articles and chapters on Polish literature, and has a forthcoming book of poetry. He teaches courses on Polish literature and culture in the Department of Modern Languages and Literatures at Loyola University Chicago. He currently lives in Champaign, Illinois, with his wife Amanda, their daughter Harriet, and their dog Leslie Knope.

www.ingramcontent.com/pod-product-compliance
Lightning Source LLC
Chambersburg PA
CBHW050909300426
44111CB00010B/1449